Betty Saw

The Asian Tofu Cookbook

Marshall Cavendish
Cuisine

The Publisher wishes to thank Aktif Lifestyle, Malaysia for the loan of their crockery and utensils.

Editors: Violet Phoon and Lydia Leong

© 2002 Times Media Private Limited
© 2009 Marshall Cavendish International (Asia) Private Limited

First published as Everything Bean Curd! in 2002

Published by Marshall Cavendish Cuisine
An imprint of Marshall Cavendish International
1 New Industrial Road, Singapore 536196

Other Marshall Cavendish Offices:
Marshall Cavendish Ltd. 5th Floor, 32-38 Saffron Hill, London EC1N 8FH, UK • Marshall Cavendish
Corporation. 99 White Plains Road, Tarrytown NY 10591-9001, USA • Marshall Cavendish
International (Thailand) Co Ltd. 253 Asoke, 12th Flr, Sukhumvit 21 Road, Klongtoey Nua, Wattana,
Bangkok 10110, Thailand • Marshall Cavendish (Malaysia) Sdn Bhd, Times Subang, Lot 46, Subang
Hi-Tech Industrial Park, Batu Tiga, 40000 Shah Alam, Selangor Darul Ehsan, Malaysia

Marshall Cavendish is a trademark of Times Publishing Limited

National Library Board Singapore Cataloguing in Publication Data

Saw, Betty.
The Asian Tofu Cookbook / Betty Saw. Singapore : Marshall Cavendish Cuisine, c2009.
p. cm.
Includes index.
ISBN-13 : 978-981-261-864-1
ISBN-10 : 981-261-864-3
1. Cookery (Tofu) I. Title.

TX814.5.T63
641.65655 -- dc22   OCN297205615

Printed in Singapore by Times Graphics Pte Ltd

*T*o Dearest Choo Boon

*T*hank you for your valued assistance

Ah Lan
Christine Ng
Jenhor Siow
Mabel Wee
Mary Lim
Phang Mee Yan

CONTENTS

JUST TOFU

TOFU AND MUSHROOMS

CONTENTS

TOFU AND CHICKEN

TOFU AND SEAFOOD

TOFU AND VEGETABLES

CONTENTS

SOUPS

CURRIES AND SAMBALS

CONTENTS

A TASTE OF TOFU : RICE AND NOODLE DISHES

*M*y kitchen experiments with tofu and other soy bean products began in earnest when, in my early 40s, a Japanese friend impressed upon me the healthy diet of the Japanese. High in soy bean products such as tofu, miso and shoyu, this diet apparently also contributed to the longevity of the Japanese in Okinawa who eat at least one or two servings of tofu daily.

Tofu promises to be an exciting new age food full of nutritional value and wholesome goodness: it is high in omega-3 oils to keep cholesterol levels down; protein-packed with essential amino acids, vitamins A, B, D and E, and brimming with calcium, iron, phosphorus, potassium and sodium. Its lecithin content helps promote healthy blood circulation and studies have shown that including soy bean foods in the diet helps reduce the risk of heart disease and cancer.

Best of all, this interesting alternative-to-meat is cheap and can be prepared in a host of cooking techniques with endless styles and recipes. Because tofu easily absorbs flavours and aromas, it is very versatile and combines wonderfully with all kinds of meat, seafood and vegetables. It can be stir-fried, deep-fried, steamed, baked, boiled or braised. Nothing beats its simplicity in preparation — just douse a steamed soft tofu with fragrant sesame oil and soy sauce and garnish with spring onions and coriander, and you have a delightful accompaniment to rice or porridge!

In writing this book, my main aim is to demonstrate how this versatile ingredient, although bland as it is, can be prepared in so many tasty ways, and at the same time, offer a healthier lifestyle choice. Although this is not a vegetarian cookbook, many of the recipes are prepared without meat and vegetarians can try these recipes by replacing meat stocks with vegetable or mushroom stocks.

I wish all my readers the joy of eating tofu!

Betty Saw

Types of Tofu and Soy Bean Products

Soft Tofu *(Taufu)*

Soft tofu, commonly known as water tofu (*suey taufu* in Cantonese), has a delicate, soft, smooth texture. It is sold in wet markets where it is cut into squares from a large slab on a wooden board. Soft tofu is ideal for mashing and steaming or used in soups. If placed in a container of cold water with a pinch of salt, it can be kept in the refrigerator for up to three days.

Variations are available. The semi-soft variety (*lam taufu*) is firm enough for cutting into cubes and can be mashed, steamed or fried. Hand-made semi-soft tofu has a slightly roundish shape, and is sold individually-wrapped in muslin cloth. You can find both hand-made and machine-made semi-soft tofu at the wet market. They are immersed in water to keep them in good shape.

A smoother type of soft tofu that has a silken texture is known as silken soft tofu. This is sold in vacuum-packed rectangular plastic boxes or wrapped tightly in a plastic roll. The tofu roll comes plain or enriched with egg, giving it a yellow colour. If refrigerated, it keeps for a couple of weeks. Use silken soft tofu for steaming or in soups and 'steamboats'. It is delicious when sliced thickly, dipped into beaten egg and flour, and deep-fried.

Pre-fried silken soft tofu (*chow lam taufu*) is available. This has a brownish exterior and can be used for steaming or braising. Before cooking, scald in boiling water to get rid of excess oil.

Firm Tofu *(Tau korn)*

Firm tofu comes in squares. It can be used whole, cut into cubes or sliced for stir-frying, braising or shallow-frying.

Compressed tofu is a solid tofu made by pressing a weight to extract water until the tofu becomes compact. It has a thinner appearance and is usually square. There is a white, plain variety and a yellow/offwhite variety flavoured with five-spice (*ng heong taufu kan*). Its smooth, resilient and meaty texture makes it ideal when sliced or diced and stir-fried with meat, seafood and vegetables, or added to curries.

Pre-fried Tofu

Pre-fried or ready-fried tofu (*chow taufu*) comes in shapes of small squares or rectangles. Soft and chewy, they are versatile and can be used for stir-frying, braising or for curries. They store well in the refrigerator and can be kept in the freezer for longer periods.

Fried tofu puffs (*taufu pok*) are puffy rounds or squares of tofu. They have a golden brown exterior with a soft, white, beehive interior. Whether plain or stuffed with meat or fish filling, the chewy texture gives it a distinctive flavour. They make delicious additions to soups and braised dishes.

Dried Bean Curd

Dried bean curd sticks (*fu chok*) and sheets are made from the dried film or skin that forms after boiling soy bean milk. The bean curd sticks add flavour to savoury and sweet soups, braised dishes, and curries. The sheets are used as wraps for meat, seafood and vegetables. Both the sticks and sheets can be stored in a cool dry place for indefinite periods.

Types of Tofu and Soy Bean Products

Sweet Bean Curd *(Tim Fu Chok)*

Sweet bean curd comes in thin rectangular pieces and is made from a thick layer of soy bean curd. It is mainly used for stir-frying with vegetables, rice or noodles and for garnish.

Fresh Layered Tofu *(Tau Pao)*

This is made from fresh wet tofu sheets, which are folded into a thick package or roll. It is wrapped in plastic and can be kept either in the refrigerator for two or three days or a few weeks in the freezer. It is usually sliced and deep-fried, braised or stewed.

Fermented Soy Bean Cake *(Tempe)*

Fermented soy bean cake has its origins in Indonesia. Wrapped in *tempe* or banana leaves or packed in plastic, it can be bought from supermarkets or Malay stalls in wet markets. Fermented soy bean cake is made from treating soaked and boiled soy beans with a fungus to initiate fermentation. It has a rich cheese-like flavour and can be added to many stir-fried dishes or curries, or eaten with sambals or chilli dips when sliced or diced and fried.

Fermented Tofu

Fermented red and white tofu are preserved in brine with rice or chillies. An acquired taste, these cubes of cheese-like tofu make pungent seasoning and are used especially in vegetarian cooking. They add zest and fragrance to vegetables. Fermented tofu is sold in glass jars: the red variety (*lam yee*) is cured in brine with red rice and sometimes seasoned with chilli, while the white variety (*fu yee*) has a creamy texture. Both varieties can be served straight from the jar as an accompaniment to plain porridge, or mashed and cooked in stir-fried and braised dishes.

Preserved Soy Beans

Preserved soy beans are made from salted fermented soy beans. They are dark brown in colour with a salty and distinctive flavour. Preserved soy beans are available as whole beans (*tau cheo*) in a thick sauce, or mashed or puréed (*tau cheong*) in glass jars. Some varieties are blended with chillies, garlic and other seasoning for a different flavour. Mainly used as condiments, in marinades and sauces, and added to stir-fried dishes, preserved soy beans give a depth of flavour and colour to stewed and braised dishes and also to roast meats.

Just Tofu

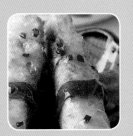

A Shoal of Tofu

The lightly spicy and tangy sauce provides an interesting contrast to the smooth and meaty texture of the tofu, making this a delightful dish.

Ingredients

Firm tofu	2 pieces, cut into 1-cm thick fingers
Salt	$^1/_2$ tsp
White pepper	$^1/_4$ tsp
Sugar	$^1/_4$ tsp
Cornflour	3 Tbsp
Egg whites	3, lightly beaten
Warm cooking oil	1 Tbsp
Oil for deep-frying	
Sunflower or olive oil	1 Tbsp
Young ginger	3 slices, peeled
Red chilli	1, seeded and chopped
Spring onions	2, cut into 4-cm lengths
Hong Kong starch or cornflour	1 tsp, mixed with 1 Tbsp water

Sauce

Fresh chicken stock*	90 ml
Salt	$^1/_2$ tsp
Sugar	$^1/_2$ tsp
White pepper	$^1/_4$ tsp
Light soy sauce	1 tsp
Cider vinegar	$^1/_2$ Tbsp

Method

- Season tofu with salt, pepper and sugar and set aside for at least 30 minutes.
- Just before frying, toss the tofu in the cornflour to coat evenly. Add the tofu to the beaten egg whites and stir in the warm cooking oil.
- Heat oil in a wok. Deep-fry the tofu until crisp and light golden. Drain on absorbent kitchen paper and set aside.
- Heat 1 Tbsp sunflower or olive oil in a clean wok and stir-fry the ginger and chilli. Return the deep-fried tofu to the wok and toss well.
- Combine the sauce ingredients, add to wok and bring to the boil.
- Add the spring onions, stir well and thicken with Hong Kong starch or cornflour mixture. Serve hot.

*Fresh Chicken Stock

Ingredients

Chicken carcasses	8, quartered and cleaned
Water	3–3$^1/_2$ litres

Method

- Boil chicken bones and water in a large, deep saucepan.
- Reduce heat and simmer, covered, over low heat for 1 hour.
- Strain the stock using a large fine sieve. Allow to cool thoroughly.
- Refrigerate or semi freeze for 2–3 hours or until oil rises and sets on the surface. Scoop off all the oil.
- Bag the stock in small portions for use as required. Stock can be frozen for several weeks. Thaw ahead of time for use as required.

Tofu Patties in Oyster Sauce

These tofu patties are great as appetisers or as part of a main meal.

Ingredients

Semi-soft tofu	2 pieces
Dried Chinese mushrooms	2, soaked to soften and finely chopped
Hong Kong starch flour for coating	
Oil for deep-frying	
Sunflower or olive oil	$^1/_2$ Tbsp
Ginger	3 thick slices, peeled
Hong Kong starch flour	2 tsp, mixed with 2 Tbsp fresh chicken stock (refer to page 18) or mushroom stock*

Seasoning

Salt	$^3/_4$ tsp
Sugar	$^1/_4$ tsp
White pepper	$^1/_4$ tsp
Egg yolk	1, small, lightly beaten
Self-raising flour	15 g

Sauce

Chicken or mushroom stock*	250 ml, fresh
Oyster sauce	1 Tbsp
Salt	$^1/_4$ tsp
White pepper	$^1/_4$ tsp

Garnish

Red chilli	1 tsp, finely chopped
Spring onions	1, chopped

Method

- Press tofu through a sieve into a bowl to mash them. Drain. Squeeze out excess water from the chopped mushrooms. Mix mushrooms with mashed tofu and seasoning. Set aside for at least 30 minutes.
- Divide mixture into 12 equal portions (each approximately 25 g) and shape into round balls. Flatten into patties. Just before frying, coat each patty with Hong Kong starch flour.
- Deep-fry in hot oil in 2 batches until golden. Drain on absorbent kitchen paper. Arrange on a serving dish.
- To prepare the oyster sauce, heat $^1/_2$ Tbsp oil in the wok and stir-fry the ginger. Combine all sauce ingredients, add to wok and bring to the boil. Thicken with Hong Kong starch flour mixture. Discard the ginger.
- Pour sauce over tofu patties. Sprinkle with chopped chillies and spring onions and serve immediately.

Note: If you coat the patties with Hong Kong starch flour, serve the dish immediately once the sauce is added. Otherwise, if left for some time, the patties will turn starchy. The patties can also be fried without coating them with Hong Kong starch flour. This way, they keep soft and spongy for a longer period of time.

To complete this dish with vegetables, scald some rosette (see picture) or baby Chinese chard and arrange them around the tofu patties before adding the sauce.

*Mushroom Stock

Mushroom stock can be made from the stems of dried Chinese mushrooms, which are usually discarded.

Ingredients

Dried Chinese mushroom stems	75 g, rinsed
Water	2 litres

Method

- Boil mushroom stems and water in a deep saucepan.
- Reduce heat and simmer, covered, for 1 hour. Strain the stock. Discard the stems.
- Allow to cool and freeze in small portions for use in soups, sauces, etc.

Tofu with Five-spice Honey Sauce

Served with rice and vegetables, this easy-to-make dish provides a simple but deliciously nutritious meal.

Ingredients

Pre-fried silken soft tofu	6 pieces
Sunflower oil	1 Tbsp

Marinade (combined)

Garlic	2 cloves, peeled and finely pounded
Young ginger	1-cm knob, peeled and finely pounded
Red chilli	$1/2$, seeded and finely chopped
Lemon juice	90 ml
Light soy sauce	2 Tbsp
Shallot oil*	$1/2$ Tbsp
Honey	3 Tbsp
Five-spice powder	$1/4$ tsp

Garnish

Spring onions	2, chopped
Coriander leaves	3 sprigs
Red chilli	6 slices

Method

- Scald tofu in boiling water to remove excess oil. Drain and place on a flat dish. Pour marinade over and set aside for 30 minutes, turning the tofu over once after 15 minutes.
- Heat sunflower oil in a non-stick pan. Reduce heat to low. Drain the tofu and fry each side for 1–2 minutes, turning over often to prevent burning.
- Add the marinade and cook over medium heat, uncovered, for 5–8 minutes or until the sauce thickens. Turn the tofu once during cooking.
- Transfer tofu to a serving dish. Pour the sauce over the tofu.
- Garnish with spring onions, coriander leaves and chillies. Serve hot.

Note: Pre-fried silken soft tofu is brown on the outside but white and silken soft inside. They are available from the wet markets.

*Shallot Oil

Ingredients

Cooking oil	375 ml
Shallots	30, peeled and thinly sliced

Method

- Heat oil in a non-stick saucepan or wok. Fry sliced shallots, stirring constantly over low heat until pale brown.
- Remove shallots with a perforated ladle to absorbent kitchen paper. When cool, store in an airtight container. They keep for several weeks in the refrigerator.
- The aromatic oil can be stored indefinitely at room temperature and can be used for steaming and stir-frying, etc. as required.

Crisp Fried Tofu Balls

These crisp tofu balls are good as party fare or as a quick snack.

Ingredients

Firm tofu	3 pieces
Tapioca flour	1$^1/_2$ Tbsp
Alkaline water	1 tsp
Medium eggs	2, lightly beaten
Small fresh Shiitake mushrooms	3, chopped
Turkey bacon (ham)	2 thin slices, chopped (optional)
Red chilli	1, seeded and chopped
Spring onion	1 Tbsp, chopped
Coriander leaves	1 Tbsp, chopped
Pinch of salt	

Method

- Press tofu through a sieve into a mixing bowl.
- Add the remaining ingredients and mix well. Use a small ice-cream scoop and shape mixture into balls. Deep-fry in hot oil at 175°C for 5–6 minutes or until golden brown.
- Serve hot.

Crispy Fermented Soy Bean Cake

Excellent as party finger food, these deep-fried soy bean cakes add crunch to any occasion.

Ingredients

Fermented soy bean cake	1 packet (240 g)
Oil for deep-frying	

Batter

Self-raising flour	55 g
Rice flour	30 g
Baking powder	$^1/_2$ tsp
Salt	1 tsp
White pepper	$^1/_4$ tsp
Turmeric powder	$^1/_2$ tsp (optional)
Water	150 ml

Garnish

Cucumber slices
Chilli sauce

Method

- Cut soy bean cake into 9 rectangles, each approximately 4.5 x 4-cm. Halve each piece horizontally.
- Preheat oil in in a deep saucepan or an electric deep-fryer to 175° C.
- Prepare the batter. Sift together self-raising flour, rice flour and baking powder into a large mixing bowl. Stir in salt, pepper and powdered turmeric (optional).
- Add water and mix until batter is smooth.
- Dip soy bean cake in batter and deep-fry in hot oil until golden brown. Drain on absorbent kitchen paper.
- Serve, garnished with cucumber slices and chilli sauce.

Note: Fermented soy bean cake (*tempe*) is popular among Indonesians. Its white fungus outer layer has a rich cheese-like flavour. It is either packed or wrapped in banana leaves or clear plastic. The plastic-packed variety was used in this recipe as it cuts into neat even rectangles.

Crispy Tofu Nuggets

These tasty nuggets are a favourite anytime.
The dips introduce a refreshing contrast of flavours.

Ingredients

Soft tofu (square)	2 pieces, cut into large cubes
Spring onion	1 Tbsp, chopped
Coriander leaves	$1/2$ Tbsp, chopped
Oil for deep-frying	

Seasoning

Sugar	$1/2$ tsp
Salt	$1/2$ tsp
White pepper	$1/4$ tsp
Sesame oil	$1/2$ tsp
Medium eggs	2, lightly beaten
Cornflour	$1/2$ Tbsp

Flour Mixture (combined)

Rice flour	1 Tbsp
Glutinous rice flour	$1^1/2$ Tbsp
Hong Kong starch flour	$1/2$ Tbsp
Baking powder	1 tsp
Pinch of white pepper	
Pinch of salt	

Method

- Place tofu cubes, a few at a time, on a small tea towel and squeeze out as much water as possible. This should give you approximately 375 g of dry tofu.
- Transfer the tofu to a mixing bowl. Add the seasoning, spring onion and coriander leaves, and stir well.
- Line an 18 x 12-cm heatproof dish with non-stick parchment paper. Fill with tofu mixture. Level the surface with the back of a spoon. Steam over rapidly boiling water for 15 minutes.
- Cool the steamed tofu thoroughly before cutting into 2.5-cm cubes.
- Just before frying, coat the tofu cubes with flour mixture.
- Heat oil in a wok. Deep-fry the tofu cubes until golden brown and crispy. Drain on absorbent kitchen paper.
- Serve with Chilli Peanut Dip*, Chilli Sesame Dip** or Spicy Mustard Tomato Sauce***.

*Chilli Peanut Dip

Ingredients

Red chillies	5, seeded
Garlic	1 Tbsp, chopped and peeled
Sugar	1 Tbsp
Lime juice	2 Tbsp
Roasted peanuts	$1/2$ Tbsp, finely ground
Salt	$1/2$ tsp

Method

- Pound chillies and garlic until fine. Add the remaining ingredients, stir well and transfer to a small sauce bowl.

** Chilli Sesame Dip

Ingredients

Red chillies	4, seeded
Cider vinegar	1 Tbsp
Sugar	1 Tbsp
Salt	$1/2$ tsp
Sesame seeds	$1/2$ Tbsp, roasted

Method

- Pound chillies until fine and put into a small pot. Add all the remaining ingredients except for the sesame seeds. Stir well and bring to a slow boil over medium heat. Stir until it thickens to a syrupy consistency. Remove from heat and add sesame seeds. Transfer to a small sauce bowl.

*** Spicy Mustard Tomato Sauce

Ingredients

Tomato sauce	2 Tbsp
Chilli sauce	1 Tbsp
Thick soy sauce	$1/2$ Tbsp
Prepared mustard	1 tsp
Sugar	1 tsp

Method

- Mix all ingredients in a bowl. Transfer to a small sauce dish.

Note: These dips/sauces go equally well with deep-fried cubes of plain semi-soft tofu or firm tofu.

Spicy Fried Tofu with Kaffir Lime Leaves

Spicy and distinctive flavours released by the dried prawn paste and aromatic kaffir lime leaves make this simple fried tofu dish very satisfying.

Ingredients

Firm tofu	4 pieces, halved and cut into 0.5-cm thick slices
Pinch of salt	
Pinch of white pepper	
Oil for deep-frying	
Fresh chicken stock	125 ml (refer to pg 18)
Kaffir lime leaves	3, finely shredded

Finely Ground

Red chillies	2, seeded
Bird's eye chillies	4, seeded
Shallots	4, peeled
Garlic	3 cloves, peeled
Dried prawn paste	2.5-cm cube
Chicken stock granules	$^1/_2$ tsp
Salt	$^1/_2$ tsp

Garnish

Spring onions	1 Tbsp, chopped

Method

- Sprinkle salt and pepper on tofu. Heat oil and deep-fry tofu until lightly browned. Drain and place on absorbent kitchen paper.
- Drain the wok, leaving 2 Tbsp of oil. Reheat the oil and stir-fry the ground ingredients over medium heat for 3–5 minutes or until fragrant. Pour in the chicken stock and bring to a quick boil. Return the fried tofu to the wok together with kaffir lime leaves. Stir to mix well.
- Dish out and serve garnished with spring onions.

Mashed Tofu in Special Sweet and Sour Sauce

This is one of my favourite versions of sweet and sour sauce. The crisp coating of the tofu cubes rapidly soaks up the tantalising caramelised sweet and piquant sauce, complementing the soft and spongy mashed tofu inside.

Ingredients

Soft tofu (square)	2 pieces, cut into large cubes
Spring onion	1 Tbsp, chopped
Coriander leaves	$1/2$ Tbsp, chopped
Oil for deep-frying	

Seasoning

Sugar	$1/2$ tsp
Salt	$1/2$ tsp
White pepper	$1/4$ tsp
Sesame oil	$1/2$ tsp
Medium eggs	2, lightly beaten
Cornflour	$1/2$ Tbsp

Flour Mixture

Rice flour	1 Tbsp
Glutinous rice flour	$1^1/2$ Tbsp
Hong Kong starch flour	$1/2$ Tbsp
Baking powder	1 tsp
Pinch of white pepper	
Pinch of salt	

Vegetables

Medium onion	1, peeled and cut into 1.5-cm squares
Red capsicum	$1/2$, cut into 1.5-cm squares
Pineapple	$1/2$ or 1 fresh piece, cut into 1.5-cm cubes or 3 rings, canned pineapple

Sauce

Chinese block brown sugar	75 g, finely chopped
Water	3 Tbsp
Brown sugar	75 g
Tomato sauce	1 Tbsp
A1 steak sauce	1 Tbsp
Cider vinegar	100 ml
Hong Kong starch flour	1 tsp, mixed with 1 Tbsp water

Method

- Place tofu cubes, a few at a time, on a small tea towel and squeeze out as much water as possible. This should give you approximately 375 g of dry tofu.
- Transfer the tofu to a mixing bowl, add seasoning, spring onion and coriander leaves and mix well.
- Line an 18 x 12-cm heatproof dish with non-stick parchment paper. Fill with tofu mixture. Level the surface with the back of a spoon. Steam over rapidly boiling water for 15 minutes.
- Cool the steamed tofu thoroughly before cutting into 2.5-cm cubes.
- Just before frying, coat the tofu cubes with flour mixture.
- Heat oil in a wok. Deep-fry the tofu cubes until golden brown and crispy. Drain on absorbent kitchen paper.
- Bring a small saucepan of water to a quick boil. Scald the onion, red capsicum and fresh pineapple for 10 seconds. Drain and set aside. If canned pineapple is used, do not scald it because scalding will reduce its sweetness.
- To prepare the sauce, heat Chinese brown sugar and water in a non-stick saucepan or wok over low heat until the sugar dissolves. Add brown sugar, mix well and then pour in tomato sauce, A1 steak sauce and cider vinegar. Stir until the sauce begins to boil and sugars dissolve.
- When the sauce thickens, add the prepared vegetables and crispy tofu cubes, stirring gently all the while. Thicken with Hong Kong starch mixture.
- Serve with rice.

Note: This versatile sweet and sour sauce is also great with meat and seafood. It can be prepared in advance and keeps well refrigerated for at least 1 week.

The steamed mashed tofu can also be prepared in advance and stored in the refrigerator for up to 3 days.

Sesame Tofu

Wonderful as a tasty snack, the deep-fried crispness of the batter contrasts with the rich velvety texture of the tofu.

Ingredients

Firm tofu	3 pieces, cut into 3 slices vertically
Egg	$1/2$, lightly beaten, mixed with 1 Tbsp milk or water
Sesame seeds	60 g
Plain flour	50 g, sifted and mixed with $1/4$ tsp salt and $1/4$ tsp white pepper
Oil for deep-frying	

Marinade

Red chilli	1, seeded and ground
Garlic	1 clove, peeled and ground
Spring onion	$1/2$, finely chopped
Light soy sauce	2 Tbsp
Chinese rice wine	5 Tbsp
Sugar	1 tsp
Salt	$1/4$ tsp
White pepper	$1/4$ tsp

Method

- Arrange tofu slices in a single layer on a flat dish.
- Combine marinade ingredients in a mixing bowl and pour over tofu. Leave to marinate for at least 15 minutes, turning the tofu slices over occasionally.
- Dip the tofu slices, one at a time, into egg and milk or water mixture. Coat with sesame seeds and flour mixture.
- Deep-fry the coated tofu slices in hot oil until golden brown. Drain on absorbent kitchen paper.
- Serve with chilli sauce.

Note: Vary the amount of sesame seeds according to your preference.

Braised Garlic Tofu

Braised tofu absorbs the aromatic fragrance of stir-fried garlic and wine to make a delicious meal with white rice.

Ingredients

Pre-fried tofu	20 pieces
Sunflower or olive oil	1 Tbsp
Garlic	20 cloves, peeled and chopped
Chinese rice wine	1 Tbsp
Pre-fried layered tofu	100 g
Red chillies	2, split
Potato flour	$1/2$ Tbsp, mixed with 1 Tbsp chicken stock (refer to page 18) or water

Stock

Fresh chicken stock	750 ml (refer to page 18)
Five-spice powder	$1/2$ tsp
Salt	$1/2$ tsp
Light soy sauce	$1^1/2$ Tbsp
Thick soy sauce	$1/2$ Tbsp
Cider vinegar	$1/2$ Tbsp
Rock sugar	$1/2$ Tbsp, crushed

Method

- Boil a saucepan of water and scald the pre-fried tofu for a minute. Drain and set aside.
- Heat oil in a saucepan and stir-fry the garlic until fragrant. Add the wine. Combine the stock ingredients. Add to saucepan and bring to the boil. Add scalded tofu and layered tofu together with chillies. When stock begins to boil again, reduce heat and simmer, covered, for 15–20 minutes or until the layered tofu is soft.
- Thicken with potato flour mixture. Serve hot.

Note: Braising allows the tofu to absorb the flavours of the garlic, wine and sauce. This dish may be prepared well in advance. Reheat before serving.

Fried Tofu in Spicy Tangy Plum Sauce

Crisp-fried shallots and an appetising but not-too-sweet piquant sauce enhances this dish.

Ingredients

Semi-soft tofu	4 pieces
Salt	1/2 tsp
Pepper	1/4 tsp
Egg	1, beaten
Potato flour for coating	
Oil for deep-frying	
Sunflower oil	1 Tbsp
Shallots	3, peeled and sliced
Garlic	3–4 cloves, peeled and chopped
Bird's eye chillies	8, chopped

Sauce

Thick plum sauce	2 Tbsp
Thai chilli sauce	2 Tbsp
Lemon juice	2 1/2 Tbsp
Chilli sauce	2 tsp
Sugar	1 tsp
Salt	1/2 tsp

Garnish

Crisp-fried shallots	1 Tbsp
Coriander leaves	1 sprig, chopped

Method

- Season tofu with salt and pepper for 15 minutes. Just before deep-frying the tofu, dip into beaten egg and coat well with potato flour.
- Meanwhile heat oil and deep-fry tofu until light golden. Arrange on a serving dish.
- Heat 1 Tbsp sunflower oil in a clean wok and lightly brown shallots and garlic. Add bird's eye chillies and sauce. Bring to the boil until slightly thickened. Pour sauce over the tofu. Garnish with crisp-fried shallots and coriander leaves.

Note: Bottled Thai chilli sauce is sweet and tangy. Thai-style chilli dip is usually made of sugar, chillies, garlic and salt. If the plum sauce is not thick enough, thicken with 1 tsp potato flour mixed with water.

Tofu &
Mushrooms

Tofu with Black Hair Moss and Straw Mushrooms

With Black Hair Moss as one of the main ingredients, this dish may be served during the Chinese New Year.

Ingredients

Semi-soft tofu	2 pieces, each cut into 16 cubes
Black hair moss	8 g, washed and soaked to soften
Gingko nuts	100 g, shelled and bitter centre shoot removed
Oil for deep-frying	
Sunflower or corn oil	2 Tbsp
Garlic	3 cloves, peeled and minced
Sweet peas	100 g, topped and tailed
Baby corn cobs	100 g, diagonally sliced
Carrots, peeled	60 g, blanched and sliced
Straw mushrooms	1 can (400 g), drained and halved
Hong Kong starch	$1^1/_2$ tsp, mixed with 2 Tbsp stock or water

Seasoning

Light soy sauce	1 tsp
Sesame oil	$^1/_2$ tsp
Salt	$^1/_4$ tsp
White pepper	$^1/_4$ tsp

Sauce

Chicken stock	175 ml (refer to page 18)
Oyster sauce	1 Tbsp
Light soy sauce	1 Tbsp
Sugar	$^1/_2$ tsp
Ginger juice	$^1/_2$ tsp
Salt	$^1/_4$ tsp
Sesame oil	1 tsp

Method

- Mix tofu cubes with seasoning gently, so as not to break them up. Set aside.
- Drain black moss and rub in 1 Tbsp sunflower or corn oil. Cook in boiling water for 2 minutes. Drain and set aside.
- Boil gingko nuts for 4–5 minutes. Drain.
- Heat oil in a deep saucepan. Deep-fry seasoned tofu for 3–5 minutes until lightly golden. Drain.
- Heat remaining sunflower or corn oil in a clean wok and lightly brown garlic. Add sweet peas, baby corn cobs and carrots and stir-fry briefly. Add straw mushrooms and mix well. Add black moss, toss well and then add gingko nuts and tofu. Stir-fry for a few seconds.
- Pour in sauce and bring to the boil. Reduce heat and simmer for 3 minutes.
- Thicken with Hong Kong starch mixture.
- Dish out and serve hot with rice.

Note: Rubbing oil into the black hair moss helps to dislodge grit and impurities clinging to the seaweed. It also helps improves the texture.

Tofu with Char Siew Mushroom Sauce

Char siew adds a sweet taste to this delicious dish.

Ingredients

Soft tofu (round)	3 pieces (150 g each), each cut into 3 even slices
Egg white	1, beaten
Plain flour	2 Tbsp
Oil for deep-frying	
Chinese chard	2–3 bunches, scalded and drained
Cooking oil	1 Tbsp
Shallots	2, peeled and sliced
Garlic	2 cloves, peeled and minced
Dried Chinese mushrooms	3, soaked to soften and diced
Canned button mushrooms	5, drained and diced
Barbecued pork or chicken	180 g, diced
Mixed frozen vegetables	1 Tbsp
Spring onion	1, chopped
Cornflour	2 tsp, mixed with 1 Tbsp water

Seasoning

Salt	$1/4$ tsp
White pepper	$1/4$ tsp
Sesame oil	1 tsp
Chinese rice wine	$1/2$ tsp

Sauce

Fresh chicken stock	175 ml (refer to page 18)
Salt	$1/4$ tsp
White pepper	$1/4$ tsp
Sugar	$1/2$ tsp
Sesame oil	1 tsp
Light soy sauce	1 tsp
Oyster sauce	1 tsp
Chinese rice wine	1 tsp

Method

- Mix tofu with the seasoning. Dip each piece in beaten egg white and coat with plain flour.
- Heat oil and fry tofu until golden. Drain and arrange on a serving dish. Arrange scalded Chinese chard around the tofu.
- Heat 1 Tbsp oil in a clean wok and lightly brown shallots and garlic. Add mushrooms and stir-fry for 30 seconds. Add the barbecued pork or chicken and toss briefly.
- Pour in the sauce and when it starts to boil, stir in the mixed vegetables and spring onion.
- Thicken with cornflour mixture, pour over the tofu and serve hot.

Tofu with Fresh Shiitake Mushrooms

A delicious and healthy stir-fry dish to accompany white rice.

Ingredients

Fresh Shiitake mushrooms	8, stemmed
Salt	$1/4$ tsp
White pepper	$1/4$ tsp
Sugar	$1/4$ tsp
Sunflower or corn oil	1 Tbsp
Shallot	1, peeled and sliced
Ginger	2 thick slices, peeled
Baby corn cobs	4, each diagonally sliced into 3
Pre-fried tofu	15 pieces, scalded
Cornflour	1 tsp, mixed with 1 Tbsp fresh chicken stock or water
Sesame oil	1 tsp
Red chilli	6–8 slices
Spring onion	1, chopped

Sauce

Fresh chicken stock	125 ml (refer to page 18)
Light soy sauce	2 tsp
Sugar	$1/4$ tsp
Salt	$1/4$ tsp

Method

- Give the mushrooms a quick rinse and season with salt, pepper and sugar.
- Heat oil in a wok and stir-fry shallots and ginger until fragrant. Add mushrooms and fry for 1 minute.
- Add corn cobs and tofu and cook for 1–2 minutes. Pour in the sauce and bring to the boil. Reduce heat and simmer for 1–2 minutes.
- Thicken with cornflour mixture. Stir in the sesame oil, chillies and spring onion before serving.

Note: Other vegetables such as broccoli, cauliflower and asparagus can also be used in place of baby corn cobs.

Claypot Tofu with Mushrooms

This classic dish has a consistency similar to shark's fin soup, but it is inexpensive to make.

Ingredients

Small prawns	90 g, shelled and deveined
Salt	$1/4$ tsp
Sugar	$1/4$ tsp
White pepper	$1/4$ tsp
Sunflower or corn oil	$1/2$ Tbsp
Chinese rice wine	1 Tbsp
Fresh Shiitake mushrooms	3, rinsed and sliced
Silken soft tofu	1 box (300 g), cut into small cubes
Potato flour	$1^1/_2$ Tbsp, mixed with 3 Tbsp stock or water
Egg whites	2, lightly beaten with 1 Tbsp water
Shallot oil	$1/2$ Tbsp (refer to page 22)
Dash of black vinegar	

Stock (combined)

Fresh chicken stock	625 ml (refer to page 18)
Salt	1 tsp
Light soy sauce	1 dsp
White pepper	$1/4$ tsp

Method

- Season prawns with salt, sugar and pepper.
- Heat oil in a medium sized claypot. Add wine and stock and bring to the boil.
- Stir in mushrooms, prawns and tofu cubes.
- When the sauce begins to boil again, thicken with potato flour mixture.
- Gradually stir in beaten egg white and water mixture and lastly, the shallot oil.
- Serve with a dash of black vinegar.

Note: A rich stock gives flavour to bland tofu. This dish is further enhanced by the flavour of the mushrooms and prawns. The acidity of the black vinegar perfectly complements the dish.

Tofu with Silver Threads and Mushrooms

Tofu and vegetables serve up a dish full of goodness.

Ingredients

Sunflower or corn oil	2 Tbsp
Garlic	2 cloves, peeled and minced
Five spice-flavoured compressed tofu	1 piece, cut into 0.5-cm thick strips
Fresh Shiitake mushrooms	100 g, rinsed
Straw mushrooms	$1/_2$ can (425 g per can), drained and rinsed
Small carrot	$1/_2$, peeled, sliced and parboiled
Snow pea	100 g, topped and tailed
Baby corn cobs	4, diagonally sliced
Red chilli	1, diagonally sliced
Transparent noodles	25 g, soaked to soften
Sesame oil	1 tsp
Potato flour	2 tsp, mixed with 2 Tbsp fresh chicken stock (refer to page 18) or water

Sauce

Fresh chicken stock	250 ml (refer to page 18)
Oyster sauce	2 tsp
Light soy sauce	2 tsp
Salt	$1/_2$ tsp
Sugar	$1/_2$ tsp
Chinese rice wine	1 tsp

Garnish

Coriander leaves

Method

- Heat oil in a wok and lightly brown garlic. Add tofu and stir-fry for 3–4 minutes. Add mushrooms and cook for 1 minute.
- Add carrot, snow peas, baby corn cobs and chilli and stir-fry for 30 seconds. Add transparent noodles
- Pour in the sauce and bring to the boil. Stir in sesame oil.
- Thicken with potato flour mixture.
- Garnish with coriander leaves and serve hot.

Note: If the Shiitake and straw mushrooms are large, halve them. Cut the transparent noodles into shorter lengths after soaking, so that they are easier to serve. As the noodles absorb the gravy after cooking, either cook the dish just before serving or add extra fresh chicken stock when ready to serve.

Five-spice Tofu with Mushroom Sauce

Mushrooms complement the aroma of the five-spice in this dish.

Ingredients

Five spice-flavoured compressed tofu	2 pieces, halved and cut into 0.75-cm thick slices
Salt	1/4 tsp
Pinch of white pepper	
Sunflower or corn oil	2 Tbsp
Shallots	2, peeled and sliced
Red chilli	1, seeded and chopped
Dried Shiitake mushrooms	4, soaked to soften and shredded
Chinese rice wine	1 tsp
Sesame oil	1 tsp
Cornflour	1 tsp, mixed with 2 Tbsp chicken stock

Sauce

Fresh chicken or mushroom stock	125 ml (refer to page 18)
Oyster sauce	1 Tbsp
Light soy sauce	1 tsp
Sugar	1 tsp
Salt	1/4 tsp

Garnish

Spring onion	1, chopped

Method

- Season tofu with salt and pepper and set aside for 5 minutes.
- Heat oil in wok and fry the tofu on both sides until lightly browned. Turn them over carefully to avoid breaking. Drain and set aside.
- Reheat oil and lightly brown shallots. Add chillies and mushrooms and cook for 1–2 minutes until fragrant. Add wine and toss for a few seconds.
- Pour in the sauce and bring to the boil. Return tofu to the wok and stir in sesame oil.
- Thicken with cornflour mixture.
- Serve, garnished with spring onion.

Note: Fresh Shiitake and button mushrooms can be used instead of the dried ones.

Fried Tofu with Leek, Mushrooms and Turkey Bacon (Ham)

Wonderful flavours from the aromatic preserved soy bean paste and smoked turkey bacon (ham) enhance this tofu dish.

Ingredients

Semi-soft tofu	3 pieces, each cut into 4 thick slices
Salt	$1/2$ tsp
White pepper	$1/4$ tsp
Plain flour for coating	
Oil for deep-frying	
Sunflower or corn oil	1 Tbsp
Garlic	2 cloves, peeled and minced
Preserved soy bean paste	1 tsp, pounded together with 1 seeded red chilli
Dried Shiitake mushroom	1, soaked to soften and shredded
Leek	30 g, diagonally sliced
Smoked turkey bacon (ham)	30 g, shredded
Red chilli	$1/2$, diagonally sliced
Cornflour	1 tsp, mixed with 2 Tbsp stock

Stock

Fresh chicken stock	175 ml (refer to page 18)
Light soy sauce	1 Tbsp
Ground rock sugar	1 Tbsp
Chinese rice wine	$1/2$ Tbsp
Salt	$1/4$ tsp
White pepper	$1/4$ tsp
Sesame oil	1 tsp

Sauce

Chicken stock	375 ml (refer to page 18)
Oyster sauce	1 Tbsp
Light soy sauce	1 Tbsp
Sugar	$1/2$ tsp
Ginger juice	$1/2$ tsp
Salt	$1/4$ tsp
Sesame oil	1 tsp
Hong Kong starch flour	$1^{1}/_{2}$ tsp, mixed with 2 Tbsp stock or water

Method

- Lightly season tofu with salt and pepper.
- Just before deep-frying, roll each piece of tofu carefully in plain flour.
- Deep-fry until light golden. Arrange on a serving plate.

To Make Sauce

- Heat sunflower or corn oil in a wok and lightly brown the garlic. Stir-fry the bean paste mixture for a few seconds.
- Add mushrooms and toss well. Add leek and cook for 30 seconds. Add turkey bacon (ham).
- Combine sauce ingredients, add to wok and bring to the boil. Add sesame oil and red chilli.
- Thicken with cornflour mixture.
- Pour over tofu and serve hot.

Prosperity Tofu and Mushrooms

This combination of black hair moss and tofu makes a propitious dish.

Ingredients

Silken soft tofu	2 rolls, cut into rounds 2-cm thick
Pinch of salt	
Sesame oil	1 tsp
Black hair moss	5 g, soaked for 10 minutes, rinsed and drained
Sunflower or corn oil	$^1/_2$ tsp
Corn oil	1 Tbsp
Fresh cloud-ear fungus	30 g, rinsed and diced
Fresh Shiitake mushrooms	4, rinsed and diced
Fresh Enoki mushrooms	1 packet (100 g), fibrous end discarded and cut into 2-cm lengths
Red chilli	1, seeded and chopped
Cornflour	1 tsp, mixed with 2 Tbsp stock or water
Sesame oil	1 tsp

Sauce

Fresh chicken stock	250 ml (refer to page 18)
Salt	$^1/_2$ tsp
White pepper	$^1/_2$ tsp
Light soy sauce	1 Tbsp

Garnish

Spring onion	1, chopped

Method

- Carefully place tofu in a heatproof dish. Sprinkle a pinch of salt and drizzle $^1/_2$ tsp sesame oil over tofu. Set aside.
- Rub $^1/_2$ tsp sesame oil and $^1/_2$ tsp sunflower or corn oil into black moss. Set aside.
- Steam the tofu over rapidly boiling water for 10 minutes. Meanwhile, heat wok and add 1 Tbsp corn oil. Briefly stir-fry cloud-ear fungus and black moss. Add mushrooms and chilli. Stir for 1 minute.
- Combine sauce ingredients, add to wok and bring to the boil. Thicken with cornflour mixture and lastly stir in 1 tsp sesame oil.
- Remove tofu from the steamer and carefully drain off the excess water. Pour the gravy over the tofu.
- Serve hot with a sprinkling of chopped spring onion.

Mushrooms with Tofu and Preserved Vegetables

A homely mix of vegetables, this dish is perfect served with a bowl of hot porridge or rice.

Ingredients

Sunflower or corn oil	3 Tbsp
Shallots	3, peeled and sliced
Preserved dried radish	90 g, rinsed and coarsely chopped
Preserved big head radish	20 g, rinsed and chopped
Fresh Shiitake mushrooms	6, rinsed and cubed
Long beans	200 g, cut into 1-cm lengths
Cauliflower	75 g, cut into tiny florets
Pre-fried tofu	12 pieces, diced
Firm tofu	1, cubed
Small red capsicum	1, cubed

Seasoning

Light soy sauce	1 Tbsp
Sugar	1 tsp
Salt	$^1/_4$ tsp
White pepper	$^1/_4$ tsp
Water	2 Tbsp

Method

- Heat oil in a wok and lightly brown shallots.
- Add both types of radish and fry for 2 minutes. Sweat the mushrooms. Add long beans and cauliflower and fry for 2 minutes.
- Add tofu and stir well. Combine seasoning ingredients and add to wok.
- Toss well and add red capsicum. Mix well. Serve with porridge or rice.

Fried Tofu Fingers with Mushrooms

The smooth creamy taste of tofu is sealed within a crisp coating in this recipe.

Ingredients

Soft tofu	600 g, mashed
Egg	1, beaten
White portion of spring onions	2, finely chopped
Coriander leaves	3 sprigs, finely chopped
Dried Chinese mushroom	1, soaked to soften and finely chopped
Small cloud ear fungus	1, soaked to soften and finely chopped
Red chilli	1, seeded and chopped
Salt	$1^1/_2$ tsp
Chicken stock granules	1 tsp
White pepper	$^1/_2$ tsp
Cornflour	2 Tbsp
Oil for deep-frying	

Coating

Egg white	1, beaten
Plain flour	

Garnish

Coriander leaves

Method

- Line a 25 x 16-cm rectangular dish with non-stick (parchment) paper.
- Combine all the ingredients except the oil, coating and garnish ingredients. Mix well. Pour into prepared dish and press down. Steam over rapidly boiling water for 10 minutes.
- Cool and cut into into 6 x 3-cm fingers. Coat with egg white and flour and deep-fry until golden. Drain on absorbent kitchen paper.
- Garnish with coriander leaves and serve.

Fried Tofu with Mushrooms and Preserved Soy Bean Paste

This simple but satisfying dish is an example of tofu transformed by the distinctive flavourful sauce of preserved soy beans.

Ingredients

Semi-soft tofu	4 pieces
Salt	$1/4$ tsp
White pepper	$1/4$ tsp
Dried Chinese mushrooms	2, soaked to soften
Sugar	$1^1/4$ tsp
White pepper	$1/4$ tsp
Light soy sauce	1 tsp
Oil for deep-frying	
Sunflower or corn oil	1 Tbsp
Thick soy sauce	2 tsp
Fresh chicken stock or water	125 ml (refer to page 18)
Red chilli	1, seeded and chopped
Spring onions	2, chopped

Finely Ground Paste

Shallots	12, peeled
Garlic	4 cloves, peeled
Preserved soy beans	$1/2$ Tbsp

Method

- Season tofu with salt and pepper.
- Chop the softened mushrooms and season with $1/4$ tsp sugar, pepper and light soy sauce.
- Heat oil in a wok and deep-fry tofu until golden brown. Drain.
- Cut each tofu into 4 pieces and arrange on serving dish.
- Heat 1 Tbsp oil in a clean wok. Stir-fry finely ground paste over medium heat until aromatic. Add seasoned mushrooms and fry for 1–2 minutes. Add the remaining sugar and thick soy sauce and stir well.
- Add stock or water and bring to a quick boil. Reduce heat and simmer for 3 minutes or until sauce thickens slightly. Stir in chilli and spring onions.
- Pour sauce over tofu and serve hot.

Tofu & Chicken

Tofu and Chicken with Sichuan Vegetables

Crunchy, spicy Sichuan preserved vegetables impart a distinctive flavour and new dimension in taste to tofu.

Ingredients

Firm tofu	4 pieces
Chicken fillet	100 g, minced
Salt	1/2 tsp
White pepper	1/4 tsp
Sichuan preserved vegetables	120 g, coarsely chopped
Oil for deep-frying	
Sunflower or corn oil	1 Tbsp
Garlic	1 Tbsp, peeled and chopped
Young ginger	1 Tbsp, peeled and chopped
Chinese rice wine	2 Tbsp
Red capsicum	100 g, cut into 1-cm cubes
Red chillies	2, seeded and cut into 1-cm cubes
Sesame oil	1 tsp
Spring onion	1, cut into 1-cm lengths
Cornflour	1 tsp, mixed with 1 Tbsp water

Sauce

Fresh chicken stock	125 ml (refer to page 18)
Light soy sauce	1/2 Tbsp
Thick soy sauce	1 tsp
Sugar	1 tsp
Salt	1/2 tsp

Method

- Cut tofu into 2-cm cubes and drain in a colander. Set aside.
- Season chicken with salt and pepper and set aside.
- Soak chopped Sichuan vegetables for 10 minutes and drain.
- Heat oil and deep-fry tofu cubes until golden brown. Drain.
- Heat sunflower or corn oil in a clean wok and lightly brown garlic and ginger. Add chicken and fry until it changes colour. Add Sichuan vegetables and cook for 1 minute.
- Drizzle in wine. Combine sauce ingredients and add to wok. When sauce boils, add red capsicum and chillies and stir well.
- Add sesame oil and spring onion. Thicken with cornflour mixture and serve hot.

Note: Chicken can be substituted with pork.

Tofu and Chicken with Spicy Garlic Sauce

A delightful dish sharpened by spicy garlic sauce.

Ingredients

Semi-soft tofu	3 pieces
Chicken fillet	60 g, finely minced
Wood ear fungus	1 Tbsp pre-soaked, finely chopped
Red chilli	1, seeded and chopped
Spring onion	1, chopped
Coriander leaves	2 sprigs, chopped
Salt	$1/2$ tsp
Chicken stock granules	$1/2$ tsp
White pepper	$1/4$ tsp
Egg	1, beaten
Self-raising flour	1 Tbsp
Cornflour	1 Tbsp
Oil for deep-frying	
Garlic sauce*	

Garnish
Tender shoots of mustard green

Method

- Press tofu through a sieve into a mixing bowl. Add chicken, wood ear fungus, chilli, spring onion, coriander leaves, salt, chicken stock granules and pepper. Mix well. Add egg, self-raising flour and cornflour.
- Heat oil in a deep-fryer to 190ºC or in a deep saucepan. Using a small ice-cream scoop, make balls of mashed tofu mixture and drop into hot oil. Deep-fry for about 3–4 minutes until golden. Drain on absorbent kitchen paper. Arrange on a serving dish and garnish with mustard green.
- Pour garlic sauce over tofu and serve hot.

*Garlic Sauce

Ingredients

Sunflower or corn oil	1 Tbsp
Garlic	4 cloves, peeled and finely chopped
Red chilli	1, seeded and chopped
Dried Chinese mushrooms	2, soaked to soften and cut into strips
Spring onions	$1/2$ Tbsp chopped
Coriander leaves	$1/2$ Tbsp chopped
Green peas	$1/2$ Tbsp
Cornflour	1 Tbsp, mixed with 1 Tbsp water

Sauce

Water	125 ml
Chicken stock granules	$1/2$ tsp
Oyster sauce	1 Tbsp
Light soy sauce	1 tsp
Sesame oil	$1/2$ tsp

Method

- Heat sunflower or corn oil and lightly brown garlic. Add chilli and mushrooms. Combine sauce ingredients and add to wok. Add spring onions, coriander leaves and green peas. Thicken with cornflour mixture. Serve hot.

Tofu, Chives and Chicken

The smooth, crunchy chives and salted mustard green complement the texture of the tofu, while imparting a piquant, garlicky flavour.

Ingredients

Skinned chicken meat	50 g, shredded
Shallot oil	1 tsp (refer to page 22)
Oil for deep-frying	
Sunflower or corn oil	1 Tbsp
Firm tofu	120 g, halved horizontally and cut into 0.5-cm strips
Garlic	2 cloves, peeled and shredded
Pickled mustard green	40 g, soaked for 10 minutes and shredded
Salt	$^1/_2$ tsp
Yellow Chinese chives	100 g, cut into 3-cm lengths
Red chilli	1, seeded and shredded
Spring onion	1, cut into 3-cm lengths
Cornflour	1 tsp, mixed with 1 Tbsp water
Sesame oil	$^1/_2$ tsp

Seasoning

Light soy sauce	$^1/_4$ tsp
White pepper	$^1/_4$ tsp
Egg white	1 tsp, beaten
Cornflour	$^1/_2$ tsp

Method

- Marinate chicken with seasoning and set aside for 15 minutes. Stir in the shallot oil just before velveting chicken in oil.
- Heat oil for deep-frying in a wok until moderately hot. Scald the chicken briefly and stir carefully to separate the pieces. Drain well on absorbent kitchen paper and set aside.
- Reheat the oil and lightly fry the tofu until light golden. Drain on absorbent kitchen paper.
- Heat sunflower or corn oil in a clean wok and fry garlic, pickled mustard green and salt until fragrant. Add chives, chilli and spring onion and stir-fry briefly.
- Return chicken and fried tofu to the wok and toss well.
- Thicken with cornflour mixture. Stir in the sesame oil and serve hot.

Note: Adding a little oil to the chicken before cooking helps to separate the pieces.

Chicken and Tofu in Hoisin Sauce

A family favourite that is easy to make and goes wonderfully with plain rice.

Ingredients

Chicken thigh	1 (whole), skinned and cut into 2-cm pieces
Salt	$1/2$ tsp
White pepper	$1/2$ tsp
Dried Chinese mushrooms	4, soaked to soften and halved
Sugar	$1/4$ tsp
Sunflower or corn oil	2 Tbsp
Garlic	3 cloves, peeled and minced
Ginger	4 thick slices, peeled
Firm tofu	3 pieces, diced into 1.5-cm cubes
Small red capsicum	1, diced
Red chilli	1, seeded and diced
Cornflour	1 tsp, mixed with 1 Tbsp water
Coriander leaves	$1/2$ Tbsp chopped

Sauce

Fresh chicken stock	125 ml (refer to page 18)
Hoisin sauce	1 Tbsp
Oyster sauce	1 Tbsp
Salt	$1/4$ tsp
Sugar	$1/2$ tsp

Method

- Season chicken with $1/4$ tsp salt and $1/4$ tsp pepper and set aside.
- Season mushrooms with $1/4$ tsp salt, $1/4$ tsp pepper and sugar. Set aside.
- Heat sunflower or corn oil in a wok and lightly brown garlic and ginger. Add chicken and cook for 1 minute. Add mushrooms and stir-fry until fragrant. Add tofu and toss gently.
- Add capsicum and chilli and mix well. Combine sauce ingredients and add to wok. Bring to the boil.
- Thicken with cornflour mixture. Add coriander leaves and serve with rice.

Chicken and Tofu with Black Beans

The flavour of aromatic fermented black beans and spring onions embraces this tofu
and chicken dish.

Ingredients

Skinned chicken meat	100 g, cut into 0.5-cm thick slices each
Semi-soft tofu	2 pieces, cut into 16 slices
Fermented black beans	1 Tbsp, rinsed
Chinese rice wine	1 Tbsp
Oil for deep-frying	
Sunflower or corn oil	1 Tbsp
Garlic	2 cloves, peeled and minced
Small leek	1 stalk, diagonally sliced
Red chilli	1, seeded and chopped
Sugar	$^1/_2$ tsp
Light soy sauce	2 tsp
Sesame oil	1 tsp

Seasoning

Thick soy sauce	$^1/_4$ tsp
Chinese rice wine	1 tsp
Cider vinegar	1 tsp
Cornflour	1 tsp

Garnish

Spring onion	1, chopped

Method

- Marinate chicken with seasoning for at least 15 minutes.
- Drain tofu in a colander.
- Combine the fermented black beans with rice wine and set aside.
- Heat oil in a saucepan and deep-fry tofu until lightly golden. Drain and set aside.
- Reheat oil and scald the chicken until just cooked. Drain and set aside.
- Heat sunflower or corn oil in a clean wok. Lightly brown garlic, then stir-fry the fermented black bean and wine mixture for a few seconds. Add leek and chilli and toss briefly.
- Return chicken and tofu to the wok. Add sugar and light soy sauce and fry until well mixed.
- Add sesame oil just before removing from wok.
- Transfer to a serving plate and garnish with chopped spring onion.

Chicken and Tofu with Dried Chillies

There are many versions of this classic Sichuan-style dish spiced with dried chillies. Here, chicken, tofu and crunchy cashew nuts make great combinations in a dark tasty sauce. If you like it less hot and fiery, shake out the seeds from the chillies after cutting them.

Ingredients

Chicken meat (thigh or breast)	250 g, skinned
Oil for deep-frying	
Sunflower or corn oil	1 Tbsp
Firm tofu	2 pieces, cut into 1.5-cm cubes
Garlic	3 cloves, peeled and minced
Dried chillies	12, rinsed and each cut into 3
Cornflour	1 tsp, mixed with 2 Tbsp water
Cashew nuts	12, roasted

Seasoning

Light soy sauce	1 dsp
Oyster sauce	1 dsp
Ginger juice	1 tsp
Water	2 Tbsp
Cornflour	2 tsp

Sauce

Light soy sauce	1 dsp
Oyster sauce	1 dsp
Worcestershire sauce	1 tsp
Sesame oil	1 tsp
Thick soy sauce	$1/2$ tsp
Sugar	1 tsp
Salt	$1/4$ tsp

Method

- Cut chicken into 2-cm cubes. Marinate with seasoning for at least 20 minutes.
- Heat oil in a wok and deep-fry tofu cubes until light golden. Drain on absorbent kitchen paper.
- Reheat the oil and deep-fry the marinated chicken for 1 minute. Drain on absorbent kitchen paper and set aside.
- Heat sunflower or corn oil in a clean wok. Stir-fry garlic and dried chillies over medium heat for 30 seconds. When the garlic is golden and fragrant, return chicken to the wok. Toss well, then add the tofu. Combine sauce ingredients and add to wok. Stir-fry for 2 minutes. Thicken with cornflour mixture and lastly add the cashew nuts. Stir well and serve hot.

Chicken and Tofu with Spring Onions

This quick-to-cook dish is enhanced with a touch of garlic, spring onion and wine.

Ingredients

Pinch of salt	
Semi-soft tofu	3, each cut into 8 pieces
Chicken meat	100 g skinned, thinly sliced
Salt	$^1/_4$ tsp
White pepper	$^1/_4$ tsp
Oil for deep-frying	
Sunflower or corn oil	1 Tbsp
Shallots	2, peeled and sliced
Garlic	2 cloves, peeled and minced
Chinese rice wine	1 Tbsp
White portion of spring onions	6, cut into 2.5-cm lengths
Red chilli	1, diagonally sliced
Egg white	$^1/_2$, beaten
Sesame oil	$^1/_2$ tsp

Sauce

Fresh chicken stock	125 ml (refer to page 18)
Light soy sauce	1 Tbsp
Thick soy sauce	$^1/_4$ tsp
Sugar	$^1/_2$ tsp
Cornflour	$^1/_2$ tsp

Method

- Sprinkle salt on tofu and set aside.
- Season chicken with salt and pepper and set aside for at least 15 minutes.
- Heat oil in a wok and deep-fry the tofu until lightly golden. Drain on absorbent kitchen paper.
- Heat sunflower or corn oil in a clean wok and lightly brown shallots and garlic.
- Add chicken and stir-fry until it changes colour. Return fried tofu to the wok and mix well. Add Chinese rice wine.
- Combine sauce ingredients and add to wok. Bring to a quick boil. Add spring onions and chilli.
- Add beaten egg white and lastly, stir in sesame oil.
- Dish onto a serving plate and serve hot with rice.

Chicken and Tofu with Peanuts

A quick home-style dish that goes well with rice or porridge.

Ingredients

Raw peanuts	100 g, skinned
Garlic	4 cloves, peeled and lightly crushed
Salt	1 tsp
Chicken meat	100 g skinned, shredded
Light soy sauce	1 tsp
Salt	$^1/_4$ tsp
White pepper	$^1/_4$ tsp
Pre-fried tofu	100 g
Sunflower or corn oil	1 Tbsp
Garlic	3 cloves, peeled and minced
Red chilli	1, seeded and shredded
Spring onion	1, chopped
Chinese rice wine	$^1/_2$ Tbsp
Cornflour	1 tsp, mixed with 2 Tbsp water

Stock

Fresh chicken stock	175 ml (refer to page 18)
Light soy sauce	$^1/_2$ Tbsp
Sugar	1 tsp
Salt	$^1/_4$ tsp
White pepper	$^1/_4$ tsp

Method

- Put peanuts, garlic and salt in a saucepan with enough water to cover. Bring to a slow boil and simmer, covered, for 30–40 minutes or until the nuts are soft. Drain and set aside.
- Marinate chicken in light soy sauce, salt and pepper for at least 15 minutes.
- Scald tofu in boiling water for 30 seconds. Drain and cut into 0.5-cm thick strips.
- Heat sunflower or corn oil in a wok and lightly brown garlic. Add chicken and stir-fry until chicken changes colour. Add peanuts and toss to mix well. Add tofu, chilli and spring onion. Cook for a minute, then add wine. Pour in the stock and bring to the boil.
- Thicken with cornflour mixture.
- Transfer to a serving plate and serve hot with rice.

Hot and Sour Greens with Tofu and Chicken

The spicy hot piquant flavours of this dish promises to whet any appetite.

Ingredients

Chicken meat	175 g skinned, thickly sliced
Salt	$1/_2$ tsp
White pepper	$1/_4$ tsp
Pre-fried tofu	10 pieces
Tofu puffs	10 pieces
Sunflower or corn oil	1 Tbsp
Shallots	2, peeled and sliced
Garlic	2 cloves, peeled and minced
Ginger	8 thick slices, peeled
Preserved soy bean paste	1 Tbsp
Lemon grass	2 stalks, bruised
Dried chillies	10, rinsed
Dried Chinese mushrooms	4, soaked to soften
Chicken and soy bean stock*	$1^1/_2$ litres
Dried sour fruit slices	15 g, rinsed
Tamarind pulp	25 g, mixed with 125 ml water for juice
Green stems	500 g, cut into large pieces
Red chillies	4, cut diagonally into 2
Oyster mushrooms	180 g, rinsed

Seasoning

Oyster sauce	2 Tbsp
Salt	2 tsp
Sugar	2 tsp

Method

- Season chicken with salt and pepper and set aside.
- Scald all the tofu in boiling water for 1 minute to remove excess oil. Drain. Halve the tofu puffs. Set aside.
- Heat oil in a deep saucepan and lightly brown shallots, garlic and ginger. Add preserved soy bean paste and stir-fry for a minute or until fragrant. Add the lemon grass, dried chillies and Chinese mushrooms. Cook for a minute.
- Pour in chicken and soy bean stock and add dried sour fruit slices, tamarind juice and bring to the boil. Add green stems, chicken and chillies. When stock begins to boil again, put in pre-fried tofu, tofu puffs and oyster mushrooms. Combine seasoning ingredients and add to wok.
- Simmer for 1 hour until vegetables are soft. Remove dried sour fruit slices and the lemon grass.
- Serve hot with rice.

*Chicken and Soy Bean Stock

Ingredients

Chicken carcasses	5, chopped
Soy beans	60 g, rinsed
Water	2 litres

Method

- Place chicken bones, soy beans and water in a deep stock pot and bring to a slow boil. Reduce heat, cover the pot and simmer for 1 hour. Skim off the scum as it rises to the surface.
- Strain the stock and let it cool completely.
- Refrigerate for several hours or until the fat rises or coagulates on the surface. Skim off the fat and use as required or transfer to containers and freeze for future use.

Note: Good stock is prepared from at least 60 percent bones and 40 percent meat. Without the meat, the stock will not have the richness or depth of flavour.

Shredded Chicken and Tofu in Hot Bean Sauce

Whether served with white rice or steamed buns to mop up the hot bean sauce, this is
a truly mouth-watering dish.

Ingredients

Chicken meat	120 g, skinned and shredded
Oil for deep-frying	
Sunflower or corn oil	2 Tbsp
Firm tofu	2 pieces, halved and cut into thin strips
Young ginger	1 Tbsp peeled and chopped
Garlic	1 Tbsp peeled and chopped
White portion of spring onion	1 Tbsp, chopped
Bottled chilli bean sauce or hot bean sauce	1 Tbsp
Wood ear fungus	15 g, soaked to soften and shredded
Cloud ear fungus	5, soaked to soften and shredded
Chinese rice wine	1 Tbsp
Water chestnuts	5–6, peeled and shredded
Cornflour	1 tsp, mixed with 2 Tbsp water

Seasoning

Light soy sauce	2 tsp
Chinese rice wine	1 tsp
Pinch of white pepper	
Fresh chicken stock or water	1 Tbsp (refer to page 18)
Cornflour	1 tsp

Sauce

Fresh chicken stock	185 ml (refer to page 18)
Light soy sauce	1 Tbsp
Sugar	2 tsp
Sesame oil	$1/2$ tsp
Thick soy sauce	$1/2$ tsp
Black vinegar	$1^1/2$ tsp
Salt	$1/2$ tsp

Method

- Rub chicken with seasoning and set aside.
- Heat oil for deep-frying and fry the tofu strips until light golden. Drain and place on absorbent kitchen paper. Reheat oil and deep-fry the seasoned chicken for 20–30 seconds. Drain.
- Heat sunflower or corn oil in a clean wok and lightly brown ginger, garlic and spring onions. Add chilli bean sauce or hot bean sauce and toss for 30 seconds.
- Add wood and cloud ear fungus and stir-fry for 1 minute. Add Chinese rice wine and water chestnuts. Mix well.
- Return chicken and tofu to the wok and toss lightly.
- Pour in the sauce and bring to a boil. Simmer for 2–3 minutes.
- Thicken with cornflour mixture and serve hot with rice or steamed buns.

Soy Custard with Minced Chicken

This popular family dish goes well with white rice. Soy bean milk adds nutrition and flavour to the custard.

Ingredients

Minced chicken	100 g
Oyster sauce	1$\frac{1}{2}$ tsp
Light soy sauce	1$\frac{1}{2}$ tsp
Unsweetened soy bean milk	475 ml
Large eggs	2, lightly stirred
Light soy sauce	1 tsp
Salt	$\frac{1}{2}$ tsp
White pepper	$\frac{1}{4}$ tsp

Topping

Sunflower or corn oil	1 Tbsp
Garlic	3 cloves, peeled and minced
Dried Shiitake or Chinese mushrooms	3, soaked to soften and chopped
Fresh chicken stock	125 ml (refer to page 18)
Cornflour	$\frac{1}{2}$ tsp, mixed with 2 Tbsp water

Garnish

Spring onion	1, chopped
Coriander leaves	2 sprigs, chopped
Crisp-fried shallots	1 Tbsp

Method

- Season chicken with oyster sauce and light soy sauce and set aside.
- Place soy bean milk and beaten eggs in a 20-cm heatproof bowl. Mix well with a fork. Stir in soy sauce, salt and pepper.
- Steam over medium heat for 15 minutes.
- To prepare the topping: heat sunflower or corn oil in a saucepan and lightly brown garlic. Add mushrooms and stir for 1–2 minutes. Add chicken. Pour in chicken stock and bring to the boil. Thicken with cornflour mixture.
- Remove custard from steamer and spread chicken topping on the surface.
- Garnish with spring onion, coriander leaves and crisp-fried shallots.

Note: The secret to steaming a smooth egg custard is to ensure that the eggs are not beaten but lightly stirred with a fork. Timing and temperature are also critical. Steam over moderate heat and do not over-steam.

Steamed Tofu with Chicken, Salted and Century Eggs

The unusual flavours of salted and century eggs and the smooth creamy texture of soft tofu makes this a delightful accompaniment to white rice or porridge.

refer to page 22
refer to page 18

Ingredients

Silken soft tofu	2 boxes
Pinch of salt	
Shallot oil	2 tsp (refer to page 22)
Salted egg	1, boiled, egg white discarded and the egg yolk chopped
Sunflower or corn oil	1 Tbsp
Garlic	2 cloves, peeled and finely minced
Canned pickled cabbage	50 g, drained and cut into 1-cm pieces
Minced chicken	120 g, seasoned with a pinch each of salt and white pepper
Century egg	1, shelled, yolk discarded and the translucent portion diced
Potato flour	2 tsp, mixed with 2 Tbsp water

Sauce

Fresh chicken stock	250 ml (refer to page 18)
Light soy sauce	2 tsp
Oyster sauce	1 tsp
Sugar	$^1/_2$ tsp
Salt	$^1/_2$ tsp
Sesame oil	$^1/_2$ tsp

Garnish

Spring onion	$^1/_2$, chopped

Method

- Carefully transfer tofu from container to a heat-proof dish. Season with salt and shallot oil.
- Sprinkle salted egg yolk over the tofu. Steam over rapidly boiling water for 10 minutes.
- Meanwhile, prepare the sauce. Heat sunflower oil in wok and lightly brown garlic. Add pickled vegetables and cook for 30 seconds. Add seasoned minced chicken and stir-fry until chicken changes colour.
- Pour in the sauce and bring to a quick boil. Add century egg. Thicken with potato flour mixture.
- To serve, remove tofu from the steamer and drain off excess water. Pour the sauce over the tofu and garnish with chopped spring onion.

Tofu & Seafood

Tofu and Dried Prawn Fritters

These tasty morsels of finger food are quick and easy to make. They are light enough for nibbles and are great for afternoon tea or a light buffet meal.

Ingredients

Plain flour	300 g
Baking powder	1 tsp
White pepper	$^1/_4$ tsp
Egg	1, beaten
Water	430 ml
Onion	1, peeled, quartered and sliced
Spring onions	2, chopped
Coriander leaves	3 stalks, chopped
Red chillies	2, seeded and chopped
Green chilli	1, seeded and chopped
Dried prawns	45 g, rinsed and finely pounded
Dried baby shrimps	30 g, rinsed
Sugar	2 tsp
Salt	1 tsp
Firm tofu	1 piece, cut into tiny cubes
Oil for deep-frying	

Method

- Sift plain flour, baking powder and pepper into a mixing bowl. Add beaten egg and stir briefly with a fork. Gradually add water, stirring at the same time until the batter is smooth.
- Stir in all the remaining ingredients except oil.
- Heat oil in an electric deep-fryer to 175°C, or in a deep saucepan.
- Using a small ice-cream scoop or tablespoon, make balls of mixture and drop into the hot oil. Deep-fry until golden brown, approximately 6 minutes. Drain on absorbent kitchen paper.
- Serve with bottled chilli sauce.

Tofu with Prawns in Garlic Oyster Sauce

This is a dish that both is pleasing to the eye and the palate. It is ideal for entertaining as most of the preparation can be done in advance.

Ingredients

Firm tofu	3 pieces
Cornflour for dusting, mixed with a pinch each of salt and white pepper	
Sunflower or corn oil	125 ml
Ginger	2 thick slices, peeled
Garlic	2 cloves, peeled and finely minced
Potato flour	2 tsp, mixed with 2 Tbsp chicken stock (refer to page 18)

Filling

Small prawns	75 g shelled and finely minced
Salt	$1/4$ tsp
White pepper	$1/4$ tsp
Water chestnut	1, peeled and chopped
Spring onions	1 tsp, chopped
Coriander leaves	1 tsp, chopped
Dried Shiitake mushroom	1, soaked to soften and chopped
Chinese rice wine	1 tsp
Sesame oil	$1/2$ tsp
Cornflour	1 tsp

Sauce

Fresh chicken or mushroom stock	200 ml (refer to page 18 or 20)
Light soy sauce	1 Tbsp
Chinese rice wine	1 tsp
Sugar	$1/2$ tsp
Sesame oil	$1/2$ tsp

Garnish

Spring onions	1 Tbsp, chopped
Coriander leaves	3 sprigs
Red chillies	2, cut into strips

Method

- Combine all the ingredients for filling in a mixing bowl. Set aside for 15 minutes.
- Cut each tofu vertically into 3 even slices and dust with cornflour-salt-pepper mixture. Sandwich the 3 slices with prawn filling to make up 3 sets.
- Heat sunflower or corn oil in a non-stick wok. Carefully lift the sandwiched tofu with a flat spatula and lower into hot oil. Fry tofu on both sides for 8–10 minutes.
- Remove tofu gently from the wok. Leave about $1/2$ Tbsp oil in wok and lightly brown ginger and garlic. Add the sauce and bring to a slow boil. Carefully return the 3 sets of tofu to the wok. Cover, reduce heat and simmer for 3–5 minutes.
- Arrange tofu in a neat row on a rectangular serving plate.
- Reheat the wok and combine sauce ingredients. Thicken with potato flour mixture and pour over the tofu.
- Garnish with spring onions, coriander leaves and chillies and serve hot.

Braised Layered Tofu with Dried Squid

The crunch of the dried squid and the softness of the tofu gives a rich contrast of textures.

Ingredients

Dried squid	60 g, cut into 2-cm squares and rinsed
Bicarbonate of soda	1/2 tsp
Oil for deep-frying	
Firm tofu	2 pieces, diced into 1.5-cm cubes
Sunflower or corn oil	1 Tbsp
Ginger	2 thick slices, peeled
Shallots	2, peeled and sliced
Dried chillies	2, rinsed and cut into 2
Fresh cloud ear fungus	20 g, rinsed
Chinese rice wine	1 Tbsp
Pre-fried layered tofu	100 g
Cornflour	2 tsp, mixed with 2 Tbsp chicken stock (refer to page 18) or water

Stock

Fresh chicken stock	325 ml (refer to page 18)
Thick soy sauce	1 Tbsp
Light soy sauce	1 Tbsp
Sugar	1 tsp
Salt	1/2 tsp
White pepper	1/4 tsp

Method

- Immerse the dried squid in water, and stir in bicarbonate of soda. Leave to soak for 1 hour. Rinse well and drain.
- Heat oil in wok and deep-fry the tofu until golden brown. Drain on absorbent kitchen paper. Set aside.
- Heat sunflower or corn oil in a clean wok and stir-fry ginger, shallots and dried chillies until fragrant.
- Add squid and stir-fry until aromatic. Add cloud ear fungus and cook for 30 seconds. Add wine.
- Pour in the stock and bring to the boil. Add pre-fried layered tofu and fried tofu cubes. Cover, reduce heat and simmer for about 10 minutes.
- Thicken with cornflour mixture and serve hot.

Note: You can substitute pre-fried layered tofu with wet tofu. Cut them into 3-cm pieces and drain well or pat dry with absorbent kitchen paper. Deep-fry in hot oil until crisp and golden brown. They store well in the refrigerator for several weeks.

Fresh cloud ear fungus is readily available in hypermarkets. If not available, substitute with 8–10 small pieces of dried cloud ear fungus, soaked to soften.

Crispy Mashed Tofu with Prawns

These crisp tasty bites are ideal as finger food for parties. Much of the preparation can be done in advance. Fry the tofu an hour or so before serving.

Ingredients

Soft tofu	3 pieces
Prawns	200 g, shelled, smashed with a cleaver and lightly mashed
Water chestnuts	5, peeled and minced
Yellow or green Chinese chives	50 g, chopped
Sugar	1 tsp
Salt	$1^1/_4$ tsp
White pepper	$^1/_4$ tsp
Sesame oil	1 tsp
Small egg	1, beaten
Cornflour	1 Tbsp
Oil for deep-frying	

Batter

Plain flour	150 g, sifted
Baking powder	$^3/_4$ tsp, sifted
Bicarbonate of soda	$^1/_4$ tsp, sifted
Salt	$^1/_2$ tsp
Water	250 ml
Sesame oil	1 tsp

Method

- Place tofu pieces on a tea towel and squeeze out as much water as possible. This should give you approximately 625 g of mashed tofu.
- In a basin, mix mashed tofu with all remaining ingredients except oil and ingredients for batter.
- Line an 18.5 x 30-cm heatproof rectangular dish with non-stick parchment paper.
- Pour tofu mixture into the dish. Level the surface and steam over rapidly boiling water for 15 minutes.
- Cool, turn out and cut into serving size rectangular pieces of 4 x 8-cm.
- To prepare batter, mix sifted ingredients and salt in a mixing bowl. Add water to form a smooth batter, thick enough to coat the back of a spoon. Stir in sesame oil.
- Dip each piece of steamed tofu into batter. Deep-fry in hot oil until golden. Drain on absorbent kitchen paper. Serve hot.

Fresh Scallops on Tofu

A simple but stunning presentation of a traditional tofu dish.

Ingredients

Fresh scallops	12
Chicken meat with a little fat	150 g, minced
Small prawns	150 g, shelled and minced
Water chestnuts	2, peeled and finely chopped
Red chilli	1, finely chopped
Spring onion	1, finely chopped
Coriander leaves	1 sprig, finely chopped
Soft tofu	2 pieces, cut into 12 regular pieces
Sunflower or corn oil	1 Tbsp
Cornflour	1 tsp, mixed with 1 Tbsp water

Seasoning A

Salt	$^1/_4$ tsp
White pepper	$^1/_4$ tsp
Sugar	$^1/_4$ tsp
Cornflour	$^1/_4$ tsp

Seasoning B

Sesame oil	1 tsp
Light soy sauce	$^1/_2$ tsp
Chinese rice wine	$^1/_2$ tsp
Salt	$^1/_2$ tsp
White pepper	$^1/_4$ tsp
Cornflour	1 tsp

Sauce

Fresh chicken stock	125 ml (refer to page 18)
Light soy sauce	1 tsp
Chinese rice wine	1 tsp
Oyster sauce	1 tsp
Sugar	$^1/_2$ tsp
Salt	$^1/_4$ tsp
White pepper	$^1/_4$ tsp

Method

- Season scallops with Seasoning A and set aside.
- Marinate minced chicken and prawns in Seasoning B. Add finely chopped ingredients. Leave aside for 30 minutes.
- Using a small 2.5-cm diameter biscuit cutter, carefully stamp out the centre of each piece of tofu, or use a knife to hollow out the centre. Gently lift and arrange hollowed-out tofu in a heatproof dish. Store the cut-out portions in a bowl of water, in the refrigerator, and use to make Tomato Tofu and Egg Soup or Hot and Sour Fish Tofu Soup (refer to page 115).
- Carefully fill the hollow of each tofu with 1 tsp of minced meat and prawn mixture. Top with a scallop.
- Place tofu in a dish and steam over rapidly boiling water for 8 minutes. Remove dish from steamer and carefully pour the juices into the sauce mixture.
- Heat sunflower or corn oil in the wok and add the sauce mixture. When it begins to boil, thicken with cornflour mixture. Pour over steamed tofu and serve hot.

Steamed Silken Soft Tofu with Bonito Flakes

A sprinkling of bonito flakes adds to the delicate flavour of this tofu dish.

Ingredients

Silken soft tofu	1 box
Japanese soy sauce	1 Tbsp
Bonito flakes	1 sachet (3 g)

Seasoning

Shallot oil	1 tsp (refer to page 22)
Salt	1/4 tsp
Pepper	1/4 tsp

Garnish

Spring onion	1, chopped

Method

- Carefully remove tofu from the box and place in a heatproof dish. Combine seasoning ingredients and lightly rub over tofu.
- Drizzle Japanese soy sauce over the tofu and top with bonito flakes. Steam over rapidly boiling water for 10 minutes.
- Remove from heat and garnish with spring onion.

Note: Bonito flakes are seasoned dried tuna flakes. They are available in small sachets at leading supermarkets.

Javanese Grilled Fish with Tofu Salad

This tender fried fish has a dark and tempting aromatic glaze. The chilli hot, tangy tomato dip goes well with the sweetness of the fish. Fried tofu and vegetables are a perfect accompaniment to the fish.

Ingredients

Threadfin or red snapper	1 (600 g)
Lime juice	1 Tbsp, combined with 1 tsp salt
Oil for deep-frying	
Firm tofu	3 pieces, each cut into 10 slices

Seasoning

Ginger juice	1 Tbsp
Garlic	3 cloves, peeled and finely pounded
Salt	1 tsp

Sauce For Grilling Fish

Indonesian sweet soy sauce	60 ml
Sunflower or corn oil	1 Tbsp
Coriander powder	1 Tbsp, roasted
Garlic	6 cloves, peeled and pounded
Sugar	$1/2$ tsp

Spicy Tomato Dip (mixed well)

Indonesian sweet soy sauce	60 ml
Shallot oil	1 Tbsp
Bird's eye chillies	6, sliced
Large ripe tomato	1, diced small
Shallots	4 cloves, sliced
Pinch of salt	

Garnish

Banana leaf	1
Cucumber	$1/2$, sliced
Lettuce	6–8 leaves, rinsed

Method

- Rub both inside and outside of fish with lime juice and salt mixture. Leave for 15–20 minutes, then rinse under running water.
- Heat oil in a wok and deep-fry tofu until golden brown. Drain and set aside. Reheat oil and deep-fry fish until light golden brown. Drain.
- Heat an electric table grill at 165°C. Place fish on hot grill and brush with sauce. Grill and brush each side of fish for 5 minutes.
- Line a serving dish with banana leaf and place grilled fish on top.
- Arrange lettuce, cucumber and tofu around the fish.
- Serve immediately with Spicy Tomato Dip.

Steamed Tofu with Minced Prawns

Minced prawns and water chestnuts create a wonderful blend of textures and lifts the simple tofu to extraordinary culinary heights.

Ingredients

Silken soft tofu	1 roll, cut into 10 slices
Prawns	300 g shelled, deveined and minced
Water chestnuts	2, peeled and minced
Red chilli	1, seeded and finely minced
Spring onion	1, finely chopped
Cornflour	2 tsp
Sunflower or corn oil	1 Tbsp, to be added last

Seasoning A

Salt	$^1/_4$ tsp
White pepper	$^1/_4$ tsp
Chinese rice wine	$^1/_2$ tsp
Sesame oil	$^1/_2$ tsp

Seasoning B

Salt	$^1/_2$ tsp
Pepper	$^1/_2$ tsp
Sugar	$^1/_2$ tsp
Fresh ginger juice	1 tsp
Sesame oil	$^1/_2$ tsp
Cornflour	1 tsp

Sauce

Fresh chicken stock	3 Tbsp (refer to page 18)
Sugar	$^1/_2$ tsp
Salt	$^1/_2$ tsp
Pinch of white pepper	
Sesame oil	$^1/_2$ tsp
Chinese rice wine	$^1/_2$ tsp
Light soy sauce	$^1/_2$ tsp
Cornflour	1 tsp

Garnish

Spring onions	2, chopped

Method

- Arrange tofu slices on a heatproof dish. Hollow out the centre of each slice with a teaspoon or knife. Sprinkle Seasoning A on the tofu.
- Mix together minced prawns, water chestnuts, chilli and spring onion and stir in Seasoning B.
- Dust the centre of the tofu with cornflour, then fill with prawn mixture. Steam tofu over rapidly boiling water for 10 minutes.
- Mix sauce ingredients and bring to a boil in a saucepan. Add the oil and simmer for 1–2 minutes. Pour sauce over the tofu and serve garnished with spring onions.

Steamed Soy Bean Custard with Seafood

The humble homey egg custard enriched with soy bean milk turns into a special treat with a topping laden with fresh seafood and mushrooms. The addition of Hong Kong starch flour gives the slippery smooth custard a soft spongy bounce.

Ingredients

Unsweetened soy bean milk	250 ml
Large egg	1, lightly beaten
Hong Kong starch flour	10 g
Salt	$1/4$ tsp
Sugar	$1/4$ tsp
Pinch of white pepper	
Dried white fungus	5 g, soaked to soften and cut into small pieces
Canned straw mushrooms	50 g, drained and sliced
Sunflower oil	$1/2$ Tbsp
Small prawns	50 g, shelled and diced
Fresh cooked crabmeat	60 g
Yellow or green Chinese chives	1 Tbsp, chopped
Hong Kong starch flour	1 tsp, mixed with 1 Tbsp water

Sauce

Fresh chicken stock	100 ml (refer to page 18)
Salt	$1/4$ tsp
Sugar	$1/4$ tsp
Chicken stock granules	$1/4$ tsp
Pinch of white pepper	

Method

- Place an 18 x 24-cm oval heatproof dish in a steamer. Cover and bring water in the steamer to a boil.
- Meanwhile, mix soy bean milk, beaten egg, starch flour, salt, sugar and pepper in a bowl.
- Remove the cover of the steamer and pour the soy bean milk and egg mixture into the heated dish. Stir with a wooden spatula for 5 minutes. When the soy bean milk and egg mixture is hot, replace the steamer cover. Steam over moderate heat for 12 minutes until the custard is set.
- Scald the white fungus and mushrooms in a small saucepan of boiling water. Drain and set aside.
- Heat sunflower oil in a wok and briefly fry the fungus and mushrooms. Add the prawns and crabmeat and cook for 30 seconds. Add the sauce and bring to the boil. Stir in chives and thicken with Hongkong starch flour mixture.
- Pour over the cooked soy bean milk and egg custard. Serve hot.

Braised Dried Oyster, Broccoli and Tofu

This is a rich and tasty vegetable dish with an unusual combination of two exotic foods, the flavourful dried oysters and slippery smooth gingko nuts.

Ingredients

Firm tofu	2 pieces, each cut into 9 wedges
Oil for deep-frying	
Chinese dried mushrooms	5 medium, soaked to soften
Sunflower or corn oil	1 Tbsp
Ginger	2 thick slices, peeled
Shallots,	2, peeled and sliced
Garlic	2 cloves, peeled and minced
Dried oysters	100 g, rinsed and soaked for 15 minutes
Black hair moss	5 g, soaked and drained
Gingko nuts	100 g, shelled and peeled with bitter centre stalk removed
Chinese rice wine	1 Tbsp
Broccoli	250 g, cut into florets
Cornflour	1 tsp, mixed with 2 Tbsp fresh chicken stock (refer to page 18) or water

Seasoning

Light soy sauce	1 tsp
Sesame oil	1 tsp
Sugar	$1/2$ tsp
White pepper	$1/4$ tsp

Stock

Fresh chicken stock	375 ml (refer to page 18)
Light soy sauce	1 Tbsp
Oyster sauce	1 Tbsp
Sugar	1 tsp
Salt	$1/2$ tsp
White pepper	$1/4$ tsp

Garnish

Spring onions	1 Tbsp, chopped

Method

- Drain tofu in a colander. Marinate mushrooms in the seasoning for 10 minutes. Heat oil in a wok and deep-fry tofu until golden and drain on absorbent kitchen paper.
- Heat sunflower or corn oil in a clean wok and lightly brown ginger, shallots and garlic. Add mushrooms, oysters and stir-fry for 30 seconds. Add black moss and gingko nuts and cook for another 30 seconds. Add rice wine.
- Pour in the stock and bring to the boil. Cover and steam for 5 minutes.
- Remove the cover, increase heat to high and add broccoli. Cover and cook for 1 minute. Thicken with cornflour mixture and garnish with a sprinkling of chopped spring onions.

Steamed Tofu with Salted Fish

An appetising and simple dish where aromatic salted fish is balanced with silken smooth and bland tofu. The ginger and chillies complement the assertive flavour of the fish.

Ingredients

Silken soft tofu	300 g box
Fried salted threadfin	12 g, crushed
Young ginger	3-cm knob, peeled and finely shredded
Red chilli	1, seeded and chopped
Shallot oil	1 Tbsp (refer to page 22)

Seasoning

Sesame oil	1 tsp
Salt	$^1/_4$ tsp
white pepper	$^1/_4$ tsp

Garnish

Spring onion	1, chopped

Method

- Carefully loosen the tofu from the box with a knife blade. Turn the tofu onto a heatproof dish.
- Rub the seasoning on the tofu. Sprinkle with crushed salted fish, ginger and chilli.
- Drizzle shallot oil over the surface. Steam over rapidly boiling water for 10 minutes.
- Garnish with chopped spring onion and serve.

Tofu with Preserved Prawns and Anchovies

This preserved prawns (cencaluk) and anchovy (ikan bilis) pickle is sharpened by lime juice and makes an excellent dip for fried or grilled fish.

Ingredients

Dried anchovies	100 g, cleaned, head removed, washed and drained
Preserved baby prawns (*cencaluk*)	100 g
Sugar	4 Tbsp, heaped
Soft tofu (round)	4–5 pieces
Kaffir lime leaves	4, finely shredded
Garlic	3 cloves, peeled and finely chopped
Torch ginger bud	1 small, outer petals discarded, halved and finely sliced
Ripe tomatoes	2, sliced
Cucumber	$1/2$, peeled, serrated and sliced
Carrot	75 g, peeled and shredded
Lime juice	110 ml, from 5–6 limes
Green chillies	3, cut into 0.75-cm lengths and seeded
Shallots	125 g peeled, rinsed and sliced thickly

Garnish

Mint leaves	1 small sprig
Red chilli	1, sliced

Method

- Place anchovies in a food processor and blend coarsely into flakes. Heat $1/2$ Tbsp oil in a non-stick pan and fry the anchovies until fragrant, about 3–5 minutes.
- Mix anchovies, preserved prawns and sugar in a small heatproof dish. Steam over rapidly boiling water for 20–25 minutes. Cool and chill.
- Steam tofu over rapidly boiling water for 10 minutes. Cool and chill.
- Arrange chilled tofu on an oval serving dish. Sprinkle half the shredded kaffir lime leaves and chopped garlic over the tofu. Top with half the torch ginger bud slices.
- Arrange tomato and cucumber slices and shredded carrot around the sides of the dish.
- Mix chilled anchovies and preserved prawn mixture with lime juice, green chillies and shallots. Add the remaining shredded kaffir lime leaves and torch ginger bud slices.
- Just before serving, pour mixture over the tofu. Top with mint leaves and garnish with chilli.

Tofu &
Vegetables

Braised Yam and Tofu in Red Fermented Tofu Sauce

A delightful family dish adapted from the famous Hakka dish, '*kao yok*'.

Ingredients

Oil for deep-frying

Yam	500 g, peeled and cut into 10 slices, each about 1-cm thick
Firm tofu	5 pieces

Sauce

Sunflower or corn oil	$^1/_2$ Tbsp
Garlic	3 cloves, peeled and chopped
Preserved soy bean paste	1 tsp
Red fermented tofu	$2^1/_2$ pieces, mashed
Five-spice powder	$^1/_2$ tsp
Chinese rice wine	1 tsp
Fresh chicken or mushroom stock	460 ml (refer to page 18 or 20)
Sugar	$1^1/_2$ tsp
Salt	$^1/_4$ tsp or to taste

Garnish

Lettuce leaves	6–8
Spring onions	2, chopped
Coriander leaves	3 sprigs, chopped

Method

- Heat oil in a wok and deep-fry yam for 3–4 minutes until just tender. Drain.
- Fry tofu until golden. Drain. Carefully halve each tofu horizontally.
- Arrange the yam, alternating with tofu, to fit snugly in a deep 19 x 7-cm round heatproof dish.
- To prepare the sauce, heat sunflower or corn oil in a wok and lightly brown garlic. Stir-fry the preserved soy bean paste and mashed red fermented tofu until aromatic. Add five-spice powder and wine.
- Pour in the chicken or vegetable stock and stir in sugar and salt. Bring to the boil, reduce heat and simmer for 2–3 minutes until aromatic.
- Pour hot sauce into the yam dish. Cover bowl with foil. Steam over rapidly boiling water for 50 minutes to 1 hour.
- Just before serving, arrange lettuce leaves in a deep round serving dish. Carefully turn the yam and tofu out onto the serving dish.
- Sprinkle with spring onions and coriander leaves.

Tofu Pakoras

These tofu and vegetable fritters are ideal for tea or as a light starter to go with drinks.

Ingredients

Chickpea flour	125 g
Meat or vegetable curry powder	1 Tbsp
Baking powder	1 tsp
Salt	1 tsp
Green chilli	1, seeded and sliced
Red chilli	1, seeded and sliced
Onion	1 large, peeled, quartered and sliced
Aubergines	75 g, quartered and sliced
Curry leaves	3 sprigs, rinsed and chopped
Water	150 ml
Firm tofu	1 piece, cut into small cubes
Oil for deep-frying	

Method

- Sift together chickpea flour, curry powder, baking powder and salt into a mixing bowl.
- Add green and red chillies, onions, aubergines and curry leaves. Gradually stir in water and mix into a batter. Add tofu cubes.
- Heat oil in an electric deep-fryer to 175°C or in a deep saucepan. Drop a tablespoonful of batter at a time, into hot oil. Deep-fry, stirring all the time until golden brown.
- Drain on absorbent kitchen paper.

Tofu and Vegetables in Mini Yam Nests

This is a dish to be savoured slowly as you dip into a yam nest of crunchy succulent vegetables.

Ingredients

Yam	400 g, peeled, diced
Cornflour	$^1/_2$ Tbsp
Vegetable shortening	45 g
Caster sugar	$1^1/_2$ Tbsp
Salt	$^1/_4$ tsp
Five-spice powder	$^1/_4$ tsp
Wheat starch	45 g, kneaded with 3 Tbsp boiling water
Oil for deep-frying	
Tofu vegetable filling*	

Garnish

Cucumber slices
Lemon slices
Coriander leaves

Method

- Steam yam for 25–30 minutes until soft. While hot, mash until fine. Add cornflour, vegetable shortening, caster sugar, salt and five-spice powder. Add wheat starch mixture and knead together.
- Refrigerate dough in a covered bowl for 30 minutes. Divide into 7 equal portions, each approximately 85 g.
- Dust a patty tin (5-cm base x 3-cm height) with cornflour and use as a mould. Press a ball of yam dough into patty tin and shape to form a small nest. Refrigerate the yam nests until needed.
- In a deep non-stick saucepan or pot, heat oil and deep-fry a couple of nests at a time until lightly golden and crisp. Remove with a wire mesh ladle and drain on absorbent kitchen paper.
- Arrange cucumber and lemon slices around the edge of a serving dish. Place yam nests in the centre and fill with tofu vegetable filling. Serve hot, garnished with coriander leaves .

*Tofu Vegetable Filling

Ingredients

Sunflower oil	1 Tbsp
Shallots	2, peeled and sliced
Garlic	2 cloves, peeled and minced
Ginger	3 thick slices, peeled
Cloud ear fungus	1 small piece, soaked to soften and diced
Water chestnuts	2, peeled and diced small
Kale stems	60 g, diced
Baby corn cobs	3, diced
Pre-fried tofu	8 pieces, diced small
Fresh or canned button mushrooms	75 g, diced
Red chilli	1, sliced
Hong Kong starch flour or cornflour	1 tsp, mixed with 2 Tbsp fresh chicken stock (refer to page 18)

Sauce

Fresh chicken or vegetable stock	125 ml (refer to page 18)
Oyster sauce	1 Tbsp
Light soy sauce	$^1/_2$ Tbsp
Sugar	1 tsp
White pepper	$^1/_4$ tsp
Sesame oil	1 tsp

Method

- Heat sunflower oil in a wok and lightly brown shallots, garlic and ginger. Add cloud-ear fungus, water chestnuts, kale stems, baby corn cobs, tofu and button mushrooms. Stir-fry for a few seconds, then stir in red chilli.
- Combine sauce ingredients and add to wok. Bring to the boil. Thicken with cornflour mixture. Remove and use as required.

Black Hair Moss Mixed Vegetables with Fermented Tofu

A healthy and scrumptious vegetable dish to serve during the Chinese New Year, with the promise of prosperity for the new year, with the use of *fatt choy*.

Ingredients

Black hair moss	8 g, soaked and well rinsed
Shallot oil	1 Tbsp (refer to page 22)
Sunflower or corn oil	3 Tbsp
Young ginger	3 slices, peeled
Shallots	3, peeled and sliced
Preserved soy bean paste	$1/2$ Tbsp
Red fermented tofu	1 piece, mashed
Fresh Shiitake mushrooms	5, rinsed and halved
Fresh cloud-ear fungus	25 g, rinsed
Chinese white cabbage	500 g, cut into 2-cm thick slices
Dried red dates	10 seeded and rinsed
Dried lily buds	20, soaked to soften and knotted individually
Dried tofu sticks	15 g, soaked to soften and cut into 3-cm lengths
Transparent noodles	25 g, soaked to soften
Pre-fried tofu	12 pieces
Potato flour	2 tsp, mixed with 2 Tbsp fresh chicken stock (refer to page 18)

Sauce

Fresh chicken stock	750 ml (refer to page 18)
Light soy sauce	1 Tbsp
Oyster sauce	1 Tbsp
Salt	1 tsp
Sugar	1 tsp
Sesame oil	1 tsp
White pepper	$1/2$ tsp

Method

- Drain the softened black moss and rub in shallot oil.
- Heat sunflower or corn oil in a deep saucepan and fry ginger and shallot until fragrant. Add soy bean paste and mashed fermented tofu and fry for a minute.
- Add mushrooms and cloud-ear fungus and stir for 2 minutes. Add the cabbage and toss until cabbage is limp.
- Combine sauce ingredients and add to wok. Bring to the boil. Add red dates, dried lily buds, dried tofu sticks, transparent noodles and pre-fried tofu. Bring to the boil again. Reduce heat and simmer, covered, for 10–12 minutes.
- Thicken with potato flour mixture. Serve hot.

Rojak Tofu with Peanut Sauce

A simple tofu salad flavoured with spicy peanut sauce. The thick sweet sauce combines the fiery flavours of three types of chillies.

Ingredients

Oil for deep frying	
Firm tofu	3 pieces
Cucumber	1/2, shredded
Baby new potatoes	5, peeled and boiled
Peanut sauce*	

Method

- Heat oil in a wok and deep-fry tofu until golden brown. Drain and place on absorbent kitchen paper.
- Just before serving, arrange shredded cucumber on the serving plate. Cut each potato into 2 and arrange on the side of the dish.
- Cut each tofu into 9 even pieces and place on the cucumbers. Pour peanut sauce over tofu and serve immediately.

*Peanut Sauce

Ingredients

Garlic	3 cloves, peeled
Red chillies	4
Green chillies	3, seeded
Dried chillies	6–8, soaked to soften and seeded
Palm sugar	45 g, chopped
Sugar	2 Tbsp
Salt	1/2 tsp
Roasted dried prawn paste granules	1 tsp
Cider vinegar	1 1/2 Tbsp
Water	125 ml
Roasted peanuts	110 g, coarsely pounded

Method

- Put all ingredients, except water and roasted peanuts, in an electric blender. Blend with a little of the water until paste is smooth.
- Pour blended ingredients into a wok. Add remaining water and bring to a slow boil. Stir and cook over low heat for about 3–5 minutes. Remove and let cool.
- Stir in pounded peanuts. Serve immediately.

Note: You can use 1 Tbsp prepared chilli paste instead of dried chillies which require time to soak and soften. To prepare and store chilli paste, slice 30 dried chillies and shake off some or all the seeds. Wash and soak in warm water for about 30 minutes. When soft, drain and purée with 125 ml water and a pinch of salt. Store in small containers or plastic bags in the freezer. The chilli paste keeps well for up to 3 months.

Stuffed Tofu Puffs with Mixed Vegetables

I have always enjoyed this simple dish served with a spicy, slightly sweet, chilli dip. There is a famous Nyonya restaurant in downtown Kuala Lumpur that does this very well. I have duplicated the recipe in my own kitchen especially for this book.

The different possibilities of vegetables such as French beans, Chinese turnips, wood ear or cloud ear fungus or other mushrooms will make equally great combinations. It is a dish that can be served as an appetiser or as part of a buffet or dinner meal. It can be prepared ahead of time. All you have to do is to reheat the stuffed tofu puffs in an oven toaster.

Ingredients

Tofu puff (square)	5 pieces
Oil for deep-frying	
Filling*	

Garnish

Cucumber slices
Tomato slices
Sweet soy sauce chilli dip**

Method

- Bring a saucepan of water to the boil and scald the tofu puffs for a few seconds to remove excess oil. Drain in a colander.
- Heat oil and deep-fry tofu puffs until crisp. Drain on absorbent kitchen paper.
- When cool, slice each tofu puff diagonally into 2 triangles. Slit each piece without cutting through and stuff with the filling.
- Arrange on a serving dish garnished with cucumber and tomato slices.
- Serve with Sweet Soy Sauce Chilli Dip.

*Filling

Ingredients

Sunflower or corn oil	1 Tbsp
Garlic	3 cloves, peeled and minced
Shallots	2, peeled and finely sliced
Fresh Shiitake mushrooms	3 (60 g), diced small
Long beans	50 g, chopped
Carrots	75 g, peeled, diced small and parboiled
Bean sprouts	100 g, tailed
Cornflour	1 tsp, mixed with 2 Tbsp fresh chicken stock (refer to page 18) or water
Spring onions	1 Tbsp, chopped
Coriander leaves	1 Tbsp, chopped

Seasoning

Salt	$1/2$ tsp
Sugar	1 tsp
Light soy sauce	1 tsp
Oyster sauce	1 tsp
White pepper	$1/4$ tsp

Method

- Heat oil in a wok and lightly brown garlic and shallots. Add mushrooms and stir-fry for a minute. Add long beans and cook for 30 seconds. Add carrots and lastly the bean sprouts. Combine seasoning ingredients and add to wok. Toss well.
- Thicken with cornflour mixture. Remove from heat and stir. Add chopped spring onions and coriander leaves. Dish out and set aside.
- Divide the filling into 5 equal portions and use as required.

**Sweet Soy Sauce Chilli Dip

Ingredients

Red chillies	3, large
Indonesian sweet soy sauce	1 Tbsp
Lemon or lime juice	1 tsp
Pinch of salt	

Method

- Blend all the ingredients in a mini food processor or blender until fine. Serve separately with stuffed tofu puffs.

Pressed Tofu, Dried Radish and Peanuts

The soft crunch of vegetables and the aromatic nutty bite of peanuts and sesame
seeds makes this an interesting and tasty dish.

Ingredients

Sunflower or corn oil	1 Tbsp
Onion	1 medium, peeled, halved and sliced
Garlic	2 cloves, peeled and minced
Dried radish	75 g, soaked for 10 minutes and chopped
Long beans	100 g, cut into 0.5-cm lengths
Carrot	75 g, peeled, diced and parboiled
Five spice-flavoured compressed tofu	100 g piece, diced
Chicken stock	2 Tbsp (refer to page 18)
Light soy sauce	2 tsp
Sugar	1 tsp
White pepper	$1/4$ tsp
Red chilli	1, seeded and diced
Peanuts	60 g, roasted
Sesame seeds	$1/2$ Tbsp, roasted

Method

- Heat oil in a wok and lightly brown onion and garlic. Add the dried radish and stir-fry for a minute. Add long beans and continue to cook for 3 minutes. Add carrot and compressed tofu.
- Add chicken stock, soy sauce, sugar, pepper and red chilli. Toss well until mixture is almost dry.
- Add peanuts and sesame seeds and mix well.
- Dish out and serve hot with rice.

Puréed Aubergine with Tofu Gems

This is a delightful dish that goes well with rice or piled on toast. The soft tofu embraces the aubergine pulp, tossed in a flavourful sauce with fragrant herbs.

Ingredients

Aubergines	600 g, peeled and thinly sliced
Salt	1 tsp
Semi-soft tofu	2 pieces, diced
Oil for deep-frying	
Sunflower oil	1 Tbsp
Garlic	4 cloves, peeled and chopped
Coriander leaves	1 Tbsp, chopped
Chinese celery leaves	1 Tbsp, chopped
Crisp-fried shallots	2 Tbsp
Sesame seeds	2 tsp, roasted
Spring onion	1, chopped

Sauce

Abalone sauce	1 Tbsp
Light soy sauce	1 Tbsp
Sesame oil	1 Tbsp
Sesame powder (refer to note)	1 Tbsp
Salt	$1/2$ tsp

Method

- Rinse the sliced aubergines in water mixed with salt. Drain and place in a heatproof dish.
- Steam over rapidly boiling water for 30 minutes or until they become very soft. Remove and drain off excess water. Cool.
- Heat oil and deep-fry tofu until lightly golden. Drain.
- Heat sunflower oil and lightly brown garlic. Combine sauce ingredients and add to wok. Stir until aubergine slices break up completely.
- Turn off the heat and add the fried tofu, coriander leaves, Chinese celery and crisp-fried shallots.
- Remove to serving dish and sprinkle with roasted sesame seeds and spring onion.

Note: Abalone sauce is an Australian product sold in bottles or jars. It is made from abalone extract, sugar, soy sauce, salt and starch. The sauce itself is ideal as a marinade or as a dip for use in stir-fries.

You can make the sesame powder by pounding or grinding 2 Tbsp roasted sesame seeds in a coffee grinder. Store in an airtight container. They keep well in the refrigerator for several weeks.

Stir-fried Tofu with Vegetables and XO Sauce

Crunchy vegetables contrast with the softness of tofu in a sweet and spicy sauce.

Ingredients

Firm tofu	2 pieces, diced into 2-cm cubes
Oil for deep-frying	
Sunflower or corn oil	$^1/_2$ Tbsp
Celery stalk	120 g, cut into 1 x 2.5-cm fingers
Carrot	60 g, peeled and cut into 1 x 2.5-cm fingers, parboiled
XO Sauce	2 Tbsp
Spring onions	2, cut into 2.5-cm lengths

Seasoning

Oyster sauce	2 Tbsp
Sesame oil	1 tsp
Ginger juice	1 tsp
Sugar	1 tsp
Cornflour	1 tsp

Method

- Mix tofu cubes with the seasoning and set aside for 15 minutes.
- Heat oil in a wok and deep-fry the tofu cubes until light golden. Drain.
- Heat $^1/_2$ Tbsp sunflower or corn oil in a clean wok and stir-fry celery for 1 minute. Add carrot and toss for another minute.
- Return tofu cubes to the wok, mix well and stir in XO Sauce and the spring onions. Serve hot.

Note: Add a couple of chopped bird's eye chillies for a fiery taste.

Stir-fried Aubergine and Tofu

Tofu soaks up the flavourful sauce of this softened aurbergine dish.

Ingredients

Aubergine	250 g, pared and cut into 1 x 5-cm chips
Sunflower or corn oil	2 Tbsp
Firm tofu	1 piece, cut into 0.5 x 5-cm strips
Shallots	2, peeled and sliced
Garlic	2 cloves, peeled and minced
Red chilli	1, seeded and coarsely chopped
Chinese rice wine	$^{1}/_{2}$ Tbsp
Cornflour	1 tsp, mixed with 1 Tbsp water

Sauce

Fresh chicken stock	125 ml (refer to page 18)
Light soy sauce	1 tsp
Oyster sauce	2 tsp
Sugar	$^{1}/_{2}$ tsp
Salt	$^{1}/_{2}$ tsp
White pepper	$^{1}/_{4}$ tsp

Garnish

Spring onion	1, chopped

Method

- Soak aubergine in salt water for 15 minutes. Drain and set aside.
- Heat oil in wok and cook aubergine for 2 minutes until just soft and lightly golden. Drain and set aside.
- Add tofu and gently fry for 1 minute. Drain and set aside.
- In the same wok, lightly brown shallots and garlic. Add chilli and return the fried aubergine and tofu to the wok. Stir-fry briefly and add rice wine. Toss well.
- Combine sauce ingredients and add to wok. Bring to the boil. Reduce heat and simmer for 2 minutes.
- Thicken with cornflour mixture. Garnish with chopped spring onions and serve hot.

Note: If the tofu is not firm enough to stir-fry, scald with hot oil for a few seconds instead.

Warm Tofu Salad with Sesame Dressing

A simple salad that makes a light and tasty meal on its own.

Ingredients

Cucumber	1 small, peeled
Firm tofu	3 pieces, cut into 1.5-cm cubes
Oil for deep-frying	
Sunflower or corn oil	1 Tbsp
Garlic	3 cloves, peeled and minced
Young ginger	2-cm knob, peeled and minced
Celery stalk	100 g, diced into 1-cm pieces
Red capsicum	$1/2$, cut into 1-cm thick slices
Cashew nuts	45 g, roasted
Sesame seeds	$1/2$ Tbsp, roasted

Sesame Dressing

Sesame oil	1 Tbsp
Light soy sauce	2 Tbsp
Cider vinegar	$3/4$ Tbsp
Sugar	$3/4$ tsp

Garnish

Spring onion	1, chopped

Method

- Quarter the cucumber lengthwise. Slice off the seeded core. Dice into 1-cm cubes and set aside.
- Heat oil and deep-fry the tofu until light golden. Drain on absorbent kitchen paper.
- Heat sunflower or corn oil in a wok and lightly brown garlic and ginger. Add celery, red capsicum and cucumber and stir-fry for a few seconds.
- Return tofu to the wok and toss well. Combine sesame dressing and add to wok. Add cashew nuts and sesame seeds. Mix well.
- Garnish with chopped spring onion.

Note: This warm salad goes well with fresh Egg Noodles in Oyster Sauce*.

*Egg Noodles in Oyster Sauce (Kon Loh Mee)

Ingredients

Fresh egg noodles	90 g per serving
Bean sprouts	50 g, tailed
Chicken (optional)	60 g, cooked and shredded

Sauce

Shallot oil	1 dsp (refer to page 22)
Oyster sauce	$1^1/2$ tsp
Thick soy sauce	1 tsp
Sesame oil	1 tsp
White pepper	$1/4$ tsp
Fresh chicken stock	2 Tbsp (refer to page 18)

Garnish

Spring onion	1, chopped

Method

- Combine sauce ingredients in a serving bowl or plate. Scald the bean sprouts and add to the sauce.
- Scald the noodles for 40–50 seconds. Drain well and plunge into cold water. Refresh in boiling water again. Drain well and place on top of bean sprouts. Mix well with sauce.
- Place shredded chicken on top and garnish with spring onion.

Note: Chicken stock adds flavour to the noodles and keeps the noodles moist.

Tofu Soups

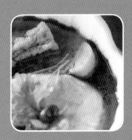

Tofu and Wakame Soup

Be seduced by the taste of the ocean released by the Wakame seaweed in
this hearty dish of healthy assorted ingredients.

Ingredients

Sesame oil	2 tsp
Leek	45 g, thinly sliced
Fresh chicken or mushroom stock	750 ml (refer to page 18 or 20)
Salt	1 tsp
Light soy sauce	1 Tbsp
Carrot	60 g, peeled and thinly sliced
Fresh Shiitake mushrooms	3, sliced
Wakame seaweed	5 g, soaked for 2 minutes
Silken soft tofu	150 g box, cut into pea-sized cubes

Garnish

Spring onion	1, chopped

Method

- Heat sesame oil in a deep saucepan and fry leek briefly.
- Pour in chicken or vegetable stock and bring to the boil. Add salt, soy sauce and carrots. Stir well and simmer for 1–2 minutes. Add Shiitake mushrooms, Wakame seaweed and tofu. Cook for 2–3 minutes. Add chopped spring onions, stir and serve hot.

Pickled Vegetable, Chicken and Tofu Soup

This is a simple soup to go with rice. Whenever I serve this at home, my husband recalls how his own mother used to make this soup.

Ingredients

Minced chicken	100 g
Salt	$^1/_4$ tsp
White pepper	$^1/_4$ tsp
Potato flour	1 tsp
Sunflower or corn oil	$^1/_2$ Tbsp
Garlic	1 clove, peeled and minced
Pickled vegetables	35 g, rinsed
Fresh chicken stock	1 litre (refer to page 18)
Salt	$1^1/_4$ tsp
Silken soft tofu	300 g box, diced
Spring onions	2 Tbsp, chopped

Method

- Season chicken with salt, pepper and potato flour and set aside for 15 minutes.
- Heat oil in a soup pot and stir-fry garlic and the pickled vegetables until fragrant. Add seasoned chicken and cook till it changes colour.
- Add chicken stock and salt. Stir, bring to the boil, reduce heat and simmer for 2–3 minutes.
- Add tofu and when stock boils again, sprinkle in spring onions. Serve hot.

Note:
Pickled vegetables are made by pickling garlic stems. They add pep and saltiness to soups while imparting a special flavour and satisfying crunch to minced meat.

The Teochews love pickled vegetables for their strong flavour. They use pickled vegetables in soups such as the popular Teochew fish ball and transparent vermicelli soup and also to steamed minced meat dishes. Transparent vermicelli and a beaten egg can also be added to this recipe.

Tofu, Mushrooms and Salted Fish Soup

The flavours released by the salted fish makes this a rich and tasty soup.

Ingredients

Shallots	5, peeled
Garlic	1 clove, peeled
Red chilli	1
Dried prawn paste	1-cm cube
Water	2–3 Tbsp
Sunflower oil	$^1/_2$ Tbsp
Fresh chicken stock	875 ml (refer to page 18)
Fresh Shiitake mushrooms	3, sliced
Fresh button mushrooms	3, sliced
Silken silken soft tofu	1 box, diced
Salted fish	25 g, fried and flaked
Salt	$^1/_4$ tsp or to taste

Garnish

Spring onion	1, chopped
Coriander leaves	3 stalks, chopped

Method

- Grind or blend shallots, garlic, chilli and dried prawn paste with 2–3 Tbsp water till fine.
- Heat sunflower oil in a soup pot and fry finely ground ingredients for 1–2 minutes or until fragrant.
- Add chicken stock and bring to the boil. Add mushrooms and tofu and bring to the boil again. Add salted fish and, if necessary, salt to taste.
- Sprinkle with chopped spring onion and coriander leaves and serve hot.

Note: If fresh button mushrooms are not available, canned straw mushrooms are a good substitute.

Fish and Tofu Soup

The culinary refinement of the famous Chinese shark's fin soup has resulted in many variations of clear, thickened soups. This one is delightful both to the palate and the eye. The delicate flavour of fresh fish and earthy mushrooms make this a tasty and nutrious soup.

Ingredients

Fish fillet	150 g (grouper, red snapper, threadfin or seabass), cut into thick slices
Salt	$1/2$ tsp
White pepper	$1/4$ tsp
Sunflower or cooking oil	$1/2$ Tbsp
Ginger	2 thick slices, peeled
Dried scallops	2 (about 20 g each), soaked to soften, shredded and drained
Fresh chicken stock	1 litre (refer to page 18)
Kale	1 thick stem, sliced
Enoki mushrooms	75 g, cut into 3-cm lengths
Soft tofu	200 g, diced small
Salt	1 tsp or to taste
Chinese rice wine	1 tsp
Potato flour	2 Tbsp, mixed 2 Tbsp water
Egg white	1, beaten

Garnish

Spring onion	1, chopped

Method

- Season fish with salt and pepper and set aside.
- Heat sunflower or cooking oil in a deep soup pot and fry ginger and scallops until fragrant. Add chicken stock and bring to the boil. Add kale stem, mushrooms, tofu and salt to taste. Add wine and simmer for 3–5 minutes.
- Thicken with potato flour mixture and stir in egg white.
- Serve soup hot, garnished with chopped spring onions.

Hot and Sour Chicken and Tofu Soup

Sichuan cuisine is robust and spicy. Its hot and sour soup is as popular as shark's fin soup. This version has an interesting mix of flavours, textures and colours with spicy, crunchy Sichuan preserved vegetable and refreshing tofu. Black vinegar and chillies add zest.

Ingredients

Skinned chicken meat	100 g, shredded
White pepper	$1/2$ tsp
Salt	$1/2$ tsp
Cornflour	$1/2$ tsp
Fresh chicken stock	$1^1/_2$ litres (refer to page 18)
Sichuan preserved vegetable	120 g, shredded
Carrot	30 g, peeled and shredded
Water chestnuts	2, peeled and shredded
Fresh Shiitake mushrooms	2, shredded
Canned straw mushrooms	100 g, drained and quartered
Red chillies	2, split
Black vinegar	3 Tbsp
Soft tofu	1 piece, shredded
Crabmeat	100 g
Potato flour	2 Tbsp, mixed with 125 ml fresh chicken stock (refer to page 18)
Egg	1, lightly beaten

Method

- Season chicken with pepper, salt and cornflour and set aside for 15 minutes.
- Boil chicken stock in a deep pot. Add Sichuan vegetable, carrot, water chestnuts, mushrooms, chillies and black vinegar. Allow to simmer for 10 minutes over low heat. Add seasoned chicken and when the soup begins to boil again, add tofu and crabmeat.
- Simmer for another 5 minutes, then stir in potato flour mixture and lastly the beaten egg. Serve hot.

Chicken, Tofu and Crispy Wantan Skin Soup

This tasty tofu soup is rich in flavour and texture.

Ingredients

Sunflower or corn oil	250 ml
Wantan wrappers	25 g, shredded 0.5-cm thick
Fresh chicken stock	$1^1/_4$ litres (refer to page 18)
Salt	1 tsp
Pinch of white pepper	
Dried Chinese mushroom	1, soaked to soften and shredded
Cloud ear fungus	1 small 5 g piece, soaked to soften and shredded
Water chestnuts	4, peeled and shredded
Firm tofu	1 piece, shredded
Egg white	1, beaten
Potato flour	3 tsp, mixed with 2 Tbsp water

Seasoned and Set Aside

Chicken meat	75 g, shredded
Salt	$^1/_4$ tsp
Cornflour	$^1/_4$ tsp
White pepper	$^1/_4$ tsp

Garnish

Spring onions	2, chopped

Method

- Heat oil in a wok and fry shredded wantan wrappers until golden brown. Remove from oil and drain.
- Boil chicken stock, salt and pepper in a large saucepan.
- When the stock comes to the boil, put in Chinese mushroom, cloud ear fungus, water chestnuts and bring to the boil again. Add seasoned chicken and shredded tofu and cook for 3–5 minutes.
- Drizzle in the beaten egg white and thicken with potato flour mixture.
- Ladle soup into soup bowls and top with wantan crisps and spring onions. Serve hot.

Note: This is easy and quick to make if you have prepared the chicken stock in advance.

Prawn and Tofu Tom Yam Soup

This spicy and tangy Thai soup makes a delicious starter to any meal.

Ingredients

Prawns	10 medium-large, eyes and feelers trimmed
Salt	1 tsp
Sunflower or corn oil	2 Tbsp
Fresh chicken, anchovy stock* or water	500 ml (chicken stock, refer to page 18)
Shallots	6, peeled and finely ground
Lemon grass	1 stalk, bruised and cut into 2-cm lengths
Ready-to-use tom yam paste	2 Tbsp
Fish sauce	2 Tbsp
Lime juice	2 Tbsp
Fresh button mushrooms	110 g, halved
Tomato	1, cut into wedges
Bird's eye' chillies	9, (6 whole, 3 sliced)
Red chilli	1, sliced
Kaffir lime leaves	2, shredded
Pre-fried soft tofu	8–10 pieces

Garnish

Coriander leaves	2 stalks

Method

- Season prawns with salt.
- Heat oil in a medium-sized heatproof casserole dish and fry prawns until they turn pink and are half-cooked. Dish out onto a plate.
- Pour chicken or anchovy stock or water into the same casserole dish and bring to the boil. Add shallots, lemon grass, tom yam paste, fish sauce, lime juice, mushrooms and tomato.
- Simmer for 20 minutes. Add the chillies, kaffir lime leaves and tofu and return prawns to the dish. Cook for 1–2 minutes.
- Remove from heat and serve hot in the casserole dish, garnished with coriander leaves.

---

*Anchovy Stock

Ingredients

Sunflower or corn oil	1 Tbsp
Dried anchovies	100 g, cleaned and rinsed
Water	$2^1/_2$–$3^1/_2$ litres

Method

- Heat oil in a deep large pot and stir-fry anchovies for 2–3 minutes.
- Pour in water and bring to a quick boil. Reduce heat and simmer, covered, for 1 hour.
- Strain the stock and let it cool. Store in small portions and freeze until required.

Seafood, Tofu and Egg Soup

A delicious soup to start any elegant meal.

Ingredients

Prawns	75 g, shelled and diced
Crabmeat	75 g, cooked
Fresh chicken stock	1 litre (refer to page 18)
Young ginger	2 thick slices, peeled
Salt	$1^1/_2$ tsp
White pepper	$^1/_4$ tsp
Silken soft tofu	1 box, diced
Chinese rice wine	1 Tbsp
Potato flour	2 Tbsp, mixed with 2 Tbsp water

Egg Mixture

Egg	1, beaten
Light soy sauce	1 tsp
Potato flour	1 tsp
White pepper	$^1/_4$ tsp

Garnish

Coriander leaves	1 Tbsp, chopped
Spring onions	1 Tbsp, chopped

Method

- Combine ingredients for egg mixture and divide into 2 portions.
- Add prawns to 1 portion of the egg mixture and crabmeat to the other. Stir and set aside.
- Bring chicken stock, ginger, salt and pepper to the boil. When the mixture boils, add tofu and stir in wine. Add the egg and prawn and egg and crabmeat mixture. When it boils again, thicken with potato flour mixture.
- Garnish with coriander leaves and spring onions. Serve hot.

Note:
Steam a crab for fresh crabmeat instead of using frozen packaged crabmeat. It may take more time, but it is well worth the effort as fresh crabmeat gives an undeniably tasty, sweet and fresh flavour to the dish.

Tomato, Tofu and Egg Soup

A simple soup that is easy on the palate.

Ingredients

Chicken or mushroom stock	1^1/$_2$ litres (refer to page 18 or 20)
Salt	1^1/$_2$ tsp
Chicken stock granules	1 tsp
Sugar	1 tsp
White pepper	^{1}/$_4$ tsp
Light soy sauce	1 Tbsp
Semi-soft tofu	2 pieces, diced small
Ripe tomatoes	240 g, peeled, seeded and diced
Spring onions	2, chopped
Eggs	2, beaten and combined with 1 tsp sesame oil

Method

- Mix chicken or mushroom stock in a large pan with salt, chicken stock granules, sugar, pepper, soy sauce, tofu and tomatoes. Stir to mix well and simmer for 2–3 minutes.
- Add spring onions and drizzle in beaten egg and sesame oil mixture. Use a fork to rake the eggs slowly into strands. Serve hot.

Hot and Sour Fish and Tofu Soup

A spicy soup heightened with the taste of lime juice and lemon grass.

Ingredients

Fish fillet	150 g (threadfin, red snapper or grouper)
Salt	1 tsp
White pepper	^{1}/$_4$ tsp
Lime juice	1 Tbsp
Sunflower or corn oil	1 Tbsp
Garlic	3 cloves, peeled and finely chopped
Lemon grass	2 stalks, crushed
Bird's eye chillies	5
Ground dried chillies	2 tsp
Ginger	2-cm knob, peeled and crushed
Fresh chicken stock	400 ml (refer to page 18)
Semi-soft tofu	1 piece, diced small
Fish sauce	1^1/$_2$ Tbsp
Kaffir lime leaves	4, finely sliced
Salt to taste	

Method

- Cut fish into 1.5-cm cubes and season with salt, pepper and lime juice. Set aside.
- Heat oil in a medium saucepan and stir-fry garlic and lemon grass. Add bird's eye chillies, ground dried chillies and ginger and cook for 1 minute.
- Add chicken stock and bring to the boil. Add tofu, fish sauce and seasoned fish cubes. Allow to boil for 5 minutes.
- Add kaffir lime leaves and salt to taste. Serve hot.

Note: The fish used in this recipe can be substituted with cuttlefish and prawns.

Curries & Sambals

Baked Prawn and Tofu Otak-otak with Sweet Basil

An exotic tofu dish distinguished by the flavour of sweet basil leaves.

Ingredients

Small prawns	100 g, shelled
Sugar	1 tsp
Salt	1½ tsp
White pepper	¼ tsp
Fresh coconut cream*	3 Tbsp
Sweet basil leaves	10 g
Large eggs	2, beaten lightly
Semi-soft tofu	2 pieces, diced small
Salam leaves	5
Lemon grass	3 stalks, smashed
Hard-boiled egg	1, shelled and chopped

Finely Ground

Candlenuts	6
Garlic	3 cloves, peeled
Turmeric	3-cm knob, peeled
Ginger	3-cm knob, peeled
Galangal	3-cm knob, peeled
Lemon grass	2 stalks, sliced

Thinly Sliced

Shallots	6, peeled
Red chillies	3
Bird's eye chillies	3
Spring onions	3

Method

- Season prawns with sugar, salt and pepper and set aside.
- Mix together finely ground ingredients, coconut cream, sliced ingredients, sweet basil leaves and eggs. Stir in prawns and tofu.
- Grease a 21 x 16-cm heatproof dish with sunflower or corn oil.
- Place the salam leaves and lemon grass at the bottom of dish and pour in prawn mixture.
- Cover the surface with a piece of foil and bake in a preheated oven at 225°C for 25 minutes.
- Serve topped with chopped hard-boiled eggs.

*To get 3 Tbsp coconut cream, squeeze approximately 175 g grated coconut using muslin cloth, without adding water.

Alternatively, packaged coconut cream is available from the wet markets and supermarkets. Use straight from the packet for thick coconut cream or mix with water as needed.

Tofu, Long Gourd and Spinach Curry

The distinctive aroma of salted threadfin enhances this mainly vegetable curry.

Sunflower or corn oil	1 Tbsp
Galangal	3-cm knob, peeled and smashed with a cleaver
Salam leaves	3–4
Sugar	1^1/$_2$ tsp
Salt	^{1}/$_2$ tsp
Water	600 ml
Low-fat milk or coconut milk	400 ml (if coconut milk, use 175 g grated coconut and 400 ml water)
Salted threadfin	90 g, rinsed, sliced thinly and pre-fried
Baby corn cobs	2, each cut into 4 pieces
Long gourd	250 g, cut into 2-cm cubes
Firm tofu	2 pieces, each cut into 6 thick slices
Baby spinach or small leaf variety spinach	200 g, cut off the roots
Coconut cream (optional)	1 Tbsp (refer to page 119)

Shallots	7, peeled
Garlic	3 cloves, peeled
Red chillies	5, seeded
Candlenuts	5
White pepper	1 tsp
Dried prawn paste granules	1 tsp, roasted
Turmeric	2-cm knob, peeled

- Heat oil and fry finely ground ingredients over low heat until fragrant, approximately 2 minutes. Add galangal, *salam* leaves and continue to cook over low heat for 8 minutes.
- Add sugar, salt, water and coconut or low-fat milk. Stir and bring to the boil. Add the salted threadfin, corn cobs, gourd and tofu. Simmer for 5–6 minutes.
- Add spinach and continue to cook until the gourd is soft. Stir in coconut cream (optional). Serve hot with rice.

Chicken and Fermented Soy Bean Cake Curry

This is a wonderfully rich curry dish that is sharpened by the fragrance of fresh kaffir lime leaves and lemon grass.

Ingredients

Chicken thigh	400 g boned, skinned and cut into 5 x 1-cm pieces
Salt	1 tsp
White pepper	$1/4$ tsp
Sunflower or corn oil	1 Tbsp
Galangal	3-cm knob, peeled and smashed
Kaffir lime leaves	5
Lemon grass	2 stalks, smashed
Salt	1 tsp
Sugar	1 tsp
Low-fat milk or coconut milk	400 ml (if coconut milk, use 175 g grated coconut and 400 ml water)
French beans	200 g, cut into 2.5-cm lengths
Ripe tomato	1, diced
Fermented soy bean cake	1 small 350 g packet, cut into 2-cm cubes and deep-fried

Finely Ground

Garlic	6 cloves, peeled
Fresh red chillies	5, seeded
Lesser galangal	$1^1/2$-cm knob, peeled
Turmeric	$1^1/2$-cm knob, peeled
Ginger	$1^1/2$-cm knob, peeled
Powdered coriander	1 Tbsp
White pepper	1 Tbsp

Method

- Season chicken with salt and pepper.
- Heat oil and sauté finely ground ingredients until fragrant. Add galangal, kaffir lime leaves, lemon grass, salt and sugar, and cook for 2 minutes.
- Add seasoned chicken and cook for 2 minutes. Stir in low-fat or coconut milk. Bring to the boil.
- Add French beans, tomato and simmer for 1–2 minutes. Add fried fermented soy bean cake and cook for 1–2 minutes. Add salt and sugar to taste. Serve hot with rice.

Chicken and Tofu Sambal

The generous amount of fresh chillies gives this rich sambal a vibrant refreshing colour. Galangal and *salam* leaves heighten the aroma.

(refer to page 119)

Ingredients

Oil for deep-frying	
Firm tofu	3 pieces, cut into 1.5-cm cubes
Galangal	3-cm knob, peeled and smashed
Salam leaves	2
Thick coconut milk	200 ml, obtained from 75 ml coconut cream and 125 ml water (refer to page 119)
Palm sugar	1 Tbsp
Sugar	1 tsp
Salt	1$^1/_2$ tsp or to taste
Mange-tout peas	50 g, topped and tailed
Baby corn cobs	4, diced
Red chillies	3, seeded and diagonally sliced

Finely Ground

Sunflower or corn oil	2 Tbsp
Red chillies	12, seeded
Shallots	6, peeled
Garlic	4 cloves, peeled
Tamarind juice	3 Tbsp, extracted and strained from 15 g tamarind pulp and 3 Tbsp water

Seasoned

Chicken	350 g, skinned and cut into 1.5-cm cubes
Salt	1 tsp
Sugar	1 tsp
White pepper	$^1/_2$ tsp

Method

- Heat oil and deep-fry the tofu until golden. Drain and set aside.
- Leaving 1 Tbsp oil in the saucepan, reheat and fry finely ground ingredients, galangal and *salam* leaves over low heat until fragrant.
- Add seasoned chicken and cook for 1 minute. Pour in coconut milk and when it comes to the boil, add palm sugar, sugar and salt to taste.
- Add the fried tofu, mange-tout peas and baby corn cobs. Add the red chillies and cook for a further 1–2 minutes until vegetables are cooked and sambal is dry. Serve with rice.

Chicken Liver with Tofu and Petai

Liver, a good source of iron, makes this a hearty and nutritious dish.

Ingredients

Oil for deep-frying	
Firm tofu	1 piece, diced small
Chicken livers	18 –20, cleaned
White pepper	$1/2$ tsp
Water	1 litre
Lemon grass	4 stalks, smashed
Galangal	5-cm knob, peeled and smashed
Salt	1 tsp
Sunflower or corn oil	2 Tbsp
Onion	1 large, peeled, halved and sliced
Garlic	2 cloves, peeled and crushed
Galangal	2-cm knob, peeled and crushed
Green chillies	5, seeded and diced into 2-cm cubes
Red chillies	3, seeded and diced into 2-cm cubes
Bird's eye chillies	4, chopped
Large red tomato	1, diced into 1-cm cubes
Petai	60 g
Salt	$1^{1}/_{2}$ tsp or to taste
Chicken stock granules	1 tsp
Indonesian sweet soy sauce	2 Tbsp
Lime juice	1 Tbsp

Garnish

Spring onion	1, cut into 1-cm lengths
Coriander	2 sprigs, cut into 1-cm lengths

Method

- Heat oil in a wok and deep-fry the firm tofu until light golden. Drain on absorbent kitchen paper. Set aside.
- Season chicken livers with pepper and set aside.
- In a large saucepan, bring water, lemon grass, galangal and salt, to the boil. Add chicken livers and cook for 2–3 minutes until livers are just cooked. Drain, cool and slice each liver into 2.
- Heat sunflower or corn oil in a pan and fry onion until soft. Add garlic and galangal and stir-fry until light brown.
- Add all the chillies and toss briefly. Add the tomato and petai. Stir in salt, stock granules, Indonesian sweet soy sauce and lime juice.
- Lastly, return tofu and chicken livers to the pan and cook until well combined.
- Dish out and serve, garnished with spring onions and coriander leaves.

Indonesian Sayur Lodeh

This is a wonderful mixed vegetable curry. If you are accustomed to lesser galangal and *petai* with their unique fragrance and flavour, then this is a curry to stir your senses and whet your appetite.

Ingredients

Coconut milk	600 ml, extracted from 175 g grated coconut and 600 ml water
Chinese turnips	100 g, peeled and cut into 4 x 1-cm fingers
Aubergine	1, roll-cut into triangles
Long beans	100 g, cut into 4-cm lengths
Baby potatoes	10, peeled and boiled for 12 minutes
Firm tofu	2 pieces, cut into 2-cm cubes
Baby corn cobs	5, diced
Petai	150 g
Small prawns	150 g, shelled
Kaffir lime leaves	2, finely sliced
Salt	1 tsp or to taste

Finely Ground

Turmeric	4-cm knob, peeled
Galangal	3-cm knob, peeled
Lesser galangal	4-cm knob, peeled
Candlenuts	4
Coriander powder	1 Tbsp
Tomato sambal*	4 Tbsp
Sunflower or corn oil	3 Tbsp

Method

- Fry finely ground ingredients in a deep saucepan over low heat, stirring all the time, until fragrant and oil rises to the surface.
- Add coconut milk and bring to a gentle boil.
- Add the turnips and aubergine, and then the long beans. Simmer for 1–2 minutes.
- Add the potatoes, tofu, baby corn cobs, *petai*, prawns and kaffir lime leaves. Stir in salt to taste.
- Simmer until the vegetables are cooked. Serve hot.

*Tomato Sambal

Ingredients

Red chillies	20, seeded
Shallots	10, peeled
Garlic	5 cloves, peeled
Dried prawn paste powder	2 tsp
Salt	1 1/2 tsp
Sunflower or corn oil	60 ml
Tomatoes	2, chopped
Sugar	1 Tbsp

Method

- Put all ingredients, except tomatoes and sugar, in a liquidiser and blend until fine. Remove and set aside. Without washing the liquidiser, put in chopped tomatoes and blend until fine. Set aside.
- In a medium saucepan, cook the blended chilli mixture over low heat, stirring all the time, until fragrant and oil appears on the surface. Add the blended tomatoes and stir-fry until sauce thickens. Stir in sugar and cook for 1 minute.
- Cool and store in an air-tight container. Tomato sambal can be stored in the refrigerator for up to 2 weeks or kept frozen for up to 3 months.

Mashed Otak-otak Tofu

A versatile dish, this can be served with white rice or used as a sandwich filling.

Ingredients

Banana leaf	1 piece
Salam leaves	4 (optional), cut into 2
Semi-soft tofu	3 pieces
Chicken meat	150 g, finely minced
Red chillies	3, seeded and thinly sliced
Green chillies	3, seeded and thinly sliced
Spring onions	2, finely chopped
Shallots	5, peeled and thinly sliced
Garlic	3 cloves, peeled and thinly sliced
Tomato sambal	2 Tbsp (refer to page 126)
Fresh coconut cream	150 ml (refer to page 119)
Egg	1, lightly beaten
Salt	1^1/$_2$ tsp

Garnish

Chillies	1, sliced
Spring onion	1, chopped

Method

- Trim banana leaf to line the base of a 16 x 27-cm heat-proof rectangular dish. Place the *salam* leaves over the banana leaf.
- Mash the tofu with a potato masher until fine. Add the rest of the ingredients and mix well. Pour mashed tofu mixture into the dish. Spread and level with the back of a spoon.
- Steam over rapidly boiling water for 20 minutes or until cooked through. Serve garnished with chillies and spring onion.

North Indian Aubergine and Tomatoes with Tofu

This is a home-style vegetable dish, flavoured with spices, and it goes well with all manner of rice dishes.

Ingredients

Sunflower or corn oil	2 Tbsp
Fennel seeds	$^1/_4$ tsp
Dried chillies	2, rinsed and each cut into 2
Onion	1, peeled and chopped
Garlic	2 cloves, peeled and chopped
Ginger	2-cm knob, peeled and grated
Tomatoes	2, diced small
Turmeric powder	$^1/_2$ tsp
Salt	$1^1/_2$ tsp
Aubergines	750 g, each sliced vertically into 6 pieces and then cut into 5-cm lengths
Fresh chicken stock or water	60 ml (refer to page 18)
Garam masala	2 tsp
Semi-soft tofu	2 pieces, diced and deep-fried
Green chilli	1, chopped
Coriander leaves	2 Tbsp, chopped

Method

- Heat oil in a wok and lightly brown fennel seeds. Add dried chillies and onion. Stir-fry for about 30 seconds until the onion is soft. Add garlic, tomatoes, turmeric and salt. Stir well, add aubergines and cook for 1 minute. Pour in stock and stir in *garam masala*.
- When stock begins to boil, add tofu, reduce heat, cover and simmer for about 5 minutes. Lastly, add green chillies and coriander leaves. Stir and serve hot.

Mushrooms and Tofu in Red Curry Paste

A 'rich' curry which is redolent of kaffir lime leaves and sweet basil, with tofu and soft mushrooms soaking in the richness and fragrance of the coconut milk.

Ingredients

Sunflower or corn oil	2 Tbsp
Onion	1, peeled and diced
Red curry paste*	125 g
Fresh chicken stock or thin coconut milk	750 ml (if chicken stock, refer to page 18, if coconut milk, extract from 175 g grated coconut and 750 ml water)
Tofu puffs	10 pieces, scalded and cut into 2.5-cm squares
Fresh Shiitake mushrooms	6, rinsed and halved
Oyster mushrooms	200 g, rinsed and halved
Fish sauce	2 Tbsp
Sugar	1 tsp
Salt	$^1/_2$ tsp or to taste
Sweet basil leaves	20
Kaffir lime leaves	3, finely shredded
Coconut cream	60 ml, extracted from 175 g grated coconut

Method

* Heat oil in a deep saucepan and fry onion until fragrant. Add red curry paste and stir-fry for 5 minutes over low heat.
* Pour in stock or thin coconut milk and bring to a boil. Add tofu, Shiitake and oyster mushrooms, fish sauce, sugar and salt. When stock begins to boil again, add basil and kaffir lime leaves and coconut cream. Stir and let it come to a gentle boil for 2–3 minutes, taking care not to overcook the mushrooms. Serve hot.

*Red Curry Paste

Ingredients

Lemon grass	3 stalks, sliced
Galangal	40 g, peeled
Dried chillies	10, soaked and seeded
Garlic	5–6 cloves, peeled
Crushed dried prawn paste or prawn paste granules	1 Tbsp
Kaffir lime leaves	2–3
Kaffir lime peel	2 tsp
Coriander roots	2
Ground white pepper	1 tsp

Method

* Blend the ingredients in an electric blender until fine.
* To store the paste, fry with 1 Tbsp sunflower or corn oil. Leave to cool. The paste can keep for 4 months in the freezer and 2 weeks in the refrigerator.

Otak-otak Chicken and Tofu

Steaming, one of the best methods of cooking, retains the flavour and juices of this dish.

Ingredients

Banana leaf	1 piece
Chicken meat	300 g, skinned
Firm tofu	2 pieces, diced
Salt	$1/2$ tsp
White pepper	$1/4$ tsp
Red chillies	2, seeded and sliced
Green chillies	3, seeded and sliced
Shallots	6, peeled and diced
Garlic	3 cloves, peeled and sliced
Thick coconut milk	200 ml, extracted from 175 g grated coconut and 200 ml water
Reserved chicken stock	50 ml (refer to method)
Salt	1 tsp
Sugar	1 tsp
Eggs	3, lightly beaten
Spring onions	2, chopped
Bird's eye chillies	5, whole

Method

- Trim the banana leaf to line the base of a 20 x 15-cm heatproof dish.
- Season chicken with half the amount of salt and pepper. Season tofu with the remaining amount. Steam separately over rapidly boiling water for 12–15 minutes until cooked through.
- Drain chicken and reserve 50 ml of the stock. Dice chicken and set aside.
- In a large mixing bowl, mix chillies, shallots and garlic. Add coconut milk, the reserved chicken stock, salt, sugar, eggs, spring onions and bird's eye chillies. Finally, add the steamed chicken and tofu. Use the back of a spoon to level the surface.
- Pour mixture into prepared dish.
- Steam over rapidly boiling water for 15 minutes. Serve hot.

Prawns and Preserved Prawns in Spicy Curry

A rich and spicy Nyonya dish, this is traditionally cooked with vegetables and preserved salted fish stomach. Here, an equally tasty alternative uses only prawns and preserved prawns (*cencaluk*).

Ingredients

Pineapple	350 g
Water	250 ml
Sunflower or corn oil	60 ml
Preserved prawns (*cencaluk*)	2 Tbsp
Medium prawns	600 g, shelled and deveined
Long beans	200 g, cut into 2-cm lengths
French beans	200 g, cut into 2-cm lengths
Torch ginger bud	2, finely sliced
Pre-fried tofu	12 pieces, scalded
Coconut cream	300 ml, extracted from 350 g grated coconut
Tamarind juice	50 g tamarind pulp mixed with 625 ml water and strained
Salt	2 tsp or to taste
Kaffir lime leaves	25
Polygonum leaves	10 stalks
Pointed pepper leaves (*daun kaduk*)	100
Mint leaves	10 stalks

Finely Ground

Dried chillies	30, cut and soaked
Lemon grass	3 stalks, sliced
Shallots	10, peeled
Torch ginger bud	4 outer petals
Galangal	1-cm knob, peeled
Dried prawn paste	1-cm square
Turmeric	1-cm knob or 1 tsp turmeric powder

Method

- Skin the pineapple and cut into wedges. Blend hard core of pineapple with 250 ml water in a liquidiser. Set aside.
- Heat oil in a deep saucepan and fry finely ground ingredients over medium heat for 5 minutes. Add preserved prawns and prawns and fry until half cooked.
- Add long beans, French beans and pineapple wedges. Toss to cook and then add the torch ginger bud. Pour in the blended pineapple mixture.
- Bring to the boil and add tofu. Add coconut cream. Simmer for 5 minutes and add tamarind juice and salt.
- Slice kaffir lime, polygonum, pepper and mint leaves finely. Rinse thoroughly, drain and mix well together. Add to simmering curry, a little at a time. Bring to the boil again and remove from heat.
- Serve with rice or vermicelli.

Note: As sap from the various leaves used can make the curry look dull, wash the finely sliced leaves well under running water before using.

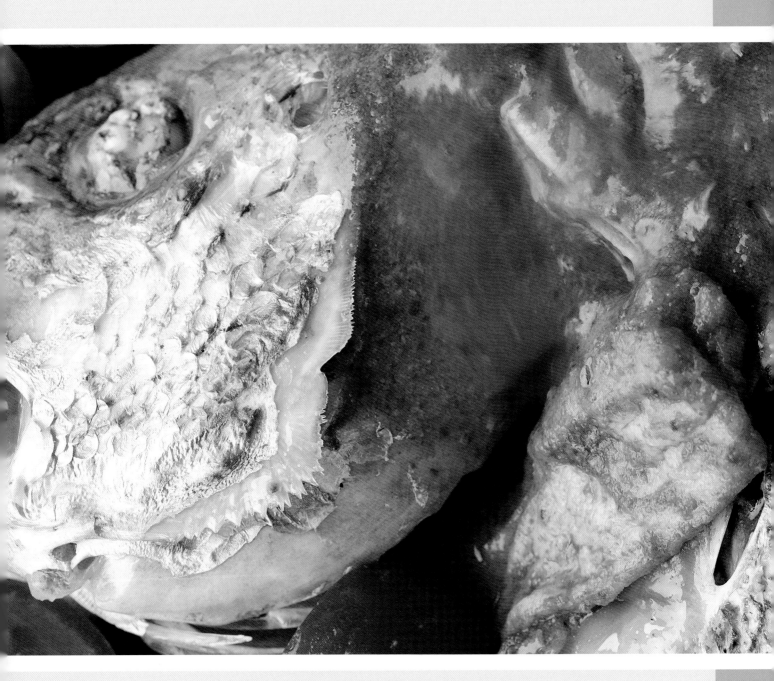

Nyonya Fish Head Curry with Tofu

A delightful aroma wafts up from the pot as you cook this curry. The wonderful fragrance of torch ginger bud and polygonum leaves seeps into the fish and tofu with their sweet and inimitable aromas.

Ingredients

Sunflower or corn oil	2 Tbsp
Lemon grass	4 stalks, smashed
Onion	1 large, peeled and cut into 6 wedges
Torch ginger bud	2, split
Tamarind juice	2 Tbsp tamarind pulp mixed with 900 ml water and strained
Polygonum leaves	12 stalks
Salt	1 1/2 tsp
Sugar	1 Tbsp
Tomatoes	2, cut into 6 wedges
Pre-fried tofu	15 pieces
Thick coconut milk	125 ml, extracted from 175 g grated coconut and 125 ml water
Torch ginger bud	1, finely sliced

Seasoned

Large fish head	1, red snapper or grouper, approximately 2 kg, halved
Salt	1 tsp
White pepper	1/2 tsp

Finely Ground

Dried chillies	15 (or 10 red chillies)
Shallots	15, peeled
Dried prawn paste	2.5-cm piece
Turmeric	2.5-cm knob, peeled

Method

- Heat oil in a large deep saucepan and fry finely ground ingredients over low-medium heat until fragrant. Add lemon grass, onion and torch ginger buds and toss well for 3 minutes.
- Pour in tamarind juice and bring to a slow boil. Add polygonum leaves, salt and sugar and simmer for 3 minutes. Add seasoned fish head and tomatoes and bring to the boil. Add pre-fried tofu and simmer for 5 minutes. Pour in thick coconut milk and add torch ginger bud. Simmer for 3 minutes. Serve hot.

Note: You can also add lady's fingers or aubergine: Steam lady's fingers (whole) or one medium aubergine (roll-cut into wedges). Add to the cooked curry.

Curry Fish Head a la Malaysia

The highlight of any meal, I have added tofu to this popular dish for additional texture.

Ingredients

Fish head	600 g (threadfin)
Salt	1 tsp
Grated coconut	350 g
Sunflower or corn oil	60 ml
Tamarind juice	20 g tamarind paste mixed with 250 ml water and strained
Lady's fingers	10
Onions	2, peeled and cut into rings
Pre-fried tofu	10 pieces, scalded and drained
Tomatoes	2, halved
Salt	1 tsp or to taste
Torch ginger bud	1, finely sliced

Finely Ground

Dried chillies	15, cut and soaked to soften
Red chillies	5
Shallots	20, peeled
Garlic	5 cloves, peeled
Turmeric	3-cm knob, peeled and sliced
Galangal	3 slices, peeled
Fennel seeds	1 Tbsp
Dried prawn paste granules	1 tsp

Method

- Halve the fish head and season with salt. Set aside.
- Using a muslin cloth, squeeze out 125 ml coconut cream from the grated coconut and set aside the cream. Add 180 ml water to the grated coconut and squeeze out 125 ml thick coconut milk. Set aside the milk.
- Heat oil in a deep saucepan and fry finely ground ingredients over medium-low heat until fragrant.
- Add tamarind juice and thick coconut milk. Bring to the boil.
- Add lady's fingers, onions, tofu and tomatoes. When the vegetables are cooked, add the fish head and cook for 5–6 minutes.
- Add coconut cream and stir in salt to taste. Turn off the heat and add sprinkling of torch ginger bud slices. Serve hot.

Salted Fish Head Curry with Tofu Puffs

This Penang Nyonya dish, packed with vegetables and tofu, is a deliciously rich curry with the fragrant aroma of salted fish.

Ingredients

Salted fish head	1, small (threadfin or snapper)
Salted fish bones	6 pieces
Grated coconut	350 g
Water	875 ml
Sunflower or corn oil	140 ml
Lemon grass	3 stalks, lightly crushed
Long beans	100 g, cut into 3.5-cm lengths
Tofu puffs (round)	10 pieces, scalded and halved
Tomatoes	2, quartered
Lemon or lime juice	2–3 tsp
Sugar	1 tsp

Finely Ground

Dried chillies	10, seeded and soaked to soften
Red chillies	5, seeded
Ginger	5-cm knob, peeled
Galangal	5-cm knob, peeled
Turmeric	5-cm knob, peeled
Shallots	150 g, peeled
Ground white pepper	1 tsp
Dried prawn paste	3-cm square

Method

- Halve the fish head and then cut again into 4 pieces. Chop the salted fish bones into serving size portions. Soak both fish head and bones in water for at least 1 hour. This reduces the salt content. Wash, drain and pat dry with absorbent kitchen paper.
- Add 125 ml water to grated coconut and extract 125 ml thick coconut milk. Set aside. Add 750 ml water to grated coconut and squeeze out 750 ml thin coconut milk.
- Heat 125 ml oil in a wok and fry salted fish until fragrant and golden brown. Drain on absorbent kitchen paper. Discard the oil.
- Heat the remaining oil in a clean wok or deep saucepan and fry finely ground ingredients and lemon grass until fragrant, approximately 8–10 minutes. Add long beans and cook for 1 minute. Pour in the thin coconut milk and bring to a slow boil. Add fish head and bones. Stir and add the tofu puffs. Let simmer for 10 minutes. Add tomatoes and cook for 2–3 minutes.
- Pour in the thick coconut milk and bring to the boil. Stir in lime juice and sugar. Add salt to taste. Serve with rice.

Note:
Salted fish bone pieces are usually taken from the backbone of salted fish after it has been filleted. The less meaty part of the tail can also be used in this dish. Aubergine and pineapples can also be added to this dish. Cut them into small pieces and add them in at the same time as the long beans.

A word of caution when adding salt—a pinch or two will usually be sufficient as the salted fish releases salt after slow simmering and cooking.

Sambal Fried Tofu with Prawns and Petai

Fresh prawns add bite to the sweet and sour flavour of this tofu sambal.

Firm tofu	4 pieces
Small prawns	150 g, shelled
Salt	$1/2$ tsp
White pepper	$1/4$ tsp
Oil for deep-frying	
Galangal	3-cm knob, peeled and crushed
Salam leaves	2
Palm sugar	1 Tbsp, chopped
Thick coconut milk	225 ml, extracted from 175 g grated coconut and 225 ml water
Petai	150 g
Red chillies	3, seeded and cut into 1-cm slices

Finely Ground

Red chillies	12, seeded
Garlic	5 cloves, peeled
Shallots	6, peeled
Salt	$1/2$ tsp
Tamarind juice	1 Tbsp tamarind pulp mixed with 3 Tbsp water and strained
Sunflower or corn oil	3 Tbsp

Method

- Cut tofu into 2-cm cubes. Drain in a colander. Set aside.
- Season prawns with salt and pepper and set aside.
- Heat oil in a saucepan and deep-fry tofu until lightly brown. Drain and set aside.
- Heat a clean saucepan and cook finely ground ingredients, without oil. Add galangal and salam leaves. Cook over low heat for 5–8 minutes or until fragrant.
- Add palm sugar and seasoned prawns and cook for 1 minute.
- Pour in coconut milk and bring to the boil. Add *petai* and chillies and stir.
- Return tofu to the pan and stir gently so as not to break them up. Serve hot.

Sambal Prawns and Tofu

Tofu and prawns are smothered in an irresistible sweet and sour sambal.

Ingredients

Medium-large prawns	250 g
Lime juice	1 Tbsp
Salt	1 tsp
White pepper	$^1/_4$ tsp
Oil for deep-frying	
Firm tofu	3 pieces, cut into 1-cm cubes
Sunflower or corn oil	2 Tbsp
Large red tomato	1, diced
Indonesian sweet soy sauce	2 Tbsp
Salt	$^1/_2$ tsp
Water	100 ml
Palm sugar	10 g, chopped
Spring onions	3, cut into 0.5-cm lengths
Kaffir lime leaves	3, finely sliced

Finelty Ground

Shallots	6, peeled
Garlic	3 cloves, peeled
Red chillies	7
Prawn paste granules	1 tsp

Method

- Trim off the eyes and feelers of the prawns. Make a slit down the centre and remove entrails. Season prawns with lime juice, salt and pepper for at least 30 minutes.
- Heat oil in a wok and deep-fry tofu until light golden. Drain on absorbent kitchen paper and set aside.
- Reheat the oil and deep-fry prawns for under a minute or until the prawns are just cooked. Drain and set aside.
- Heat sunflower or corn oil in a clean wok and stir-fry finely ground ingredients over low heat until fragrant. Add tomatoes and stir for 1 minute. Add Indonesian sweet soy sauce, salt, water and palm sugar and bring to a boil. Simmer for 1 minute or until sauce thickens.
- Return tofu and prawns to the wok and stir in chopped spring onions and kaffir lime leaves.

Note: Choose fresh prawns. Do not overcook them or they will lose their sweetness and firmness.

Sambal Fermented Soy Bean Cake Seafood

The tang of lemon grass and tamarind juice provides a unique taste to the crunch of deep-fried tofu.

Ingredients

Small prawns or cuttlefish	275 g
Salt	1 tsp
Sugar	1/4 tsp
White pepper	1/4 tsp
Oil for deep-frying	
Fermented soy bean cake	8 packets, cut into 1.5-cm cubes
Semi-soft tofu	4 pieces, cut into 1.5-cm cubes
Sunflower or corn oil	5 Tbsp
Long beans	300 g, cut into 3-cm lengths
Sugar	1 tsp
Salt	1/4 tsp
Garlic	30 g, peeled and sliced
Lemon grass	4 stalks (2 sliced, 2 bruised)
Tamarind juice	2 Tbsp tamarind pulp mixed with 125 ml water and strained
Fresh coconut cream	125 ml, mixed with 100 ml water (refer to page 119)
Sugar	2 Tbsp
Salt	1 tsp or to taste
Lime juice	1 Tbsp
Red chilli	1, seeded and sliced
Green chilli	1, seeded and sliced

Finely Ground

Red chillies	5
Shallots	120 g, peeled
Garlic	30 g, peeled

Method

- Season prawns or cuttlefish with salt, sugar and pepper. Set aside.
- Heat oil and deep-fry fermented soy bean cake and tofu separately until golden brown. Drain and set aside.
- Heat 1 Tbsp sunflower or corn oil in a wok and stir-fry prawns or cuttlefish until cooked. Remove and set aside.
- In the same wok, heat another Tbsp sunflower or corn oil and fry the long beans until soft. Add sugar and salt. Mix well and transfer to a plate.
- In a clean wok, heat remaining sunflower or corn oil and fry finely ground ingredients, garlic and lemon grass over low heat until fragrant.
- Add the tamarind juice and the coconut cream mixture. Stir and add the sugar and salt to taste. Stir over moderate heat until mixture boils.
- Add the fried long beans, fermented soy bean cakes and tofu. Increase heat and cook until almost dry. Stir in lime juice and chillies. Serve with rice.

Note: Fermented soy bean cake can be bought at wet markets. They are usually available in leaf-wrapped packets of 35 g each.

Tomato and Tofu Sambal

This easy-to-prepare dish can complement any main meal.

Ingredients

Semi-soft tofu	2 pieces, cut into 2-cm cubes
Lime juice	$^1/_2$ Tbsp
Salt	$^1/_4$ tsp
Oil for deep-frying	
Sunflower or corn oil	1 Tbsp
Medium-large tomato	1; cut into 8 wedges
Indonesian sweet soy sauce	1 Tbsp
Spring onions	2, cut into 1.5-cm lengths
Palm sugar	1 tsp, chopped
Salt	$^1/_2$ tsp
Chicken stock or water	60 ml (refer to page 18)

Finely Ground

Shallots	3, peeled
Garlic	2 cloves, peeled
Red chillies	3, seeded
Dried prawn paste granules	1 tsp

Garnish

Coriander leaves

Method

- Marinate tofu in lime juice and salt. Drain in a colander.
- Heat oil in a deep saucepan and deep-fry the tofu until golden. Drain on absorbent kitchen paper and set aside.
- Heat sunflower or corn oil in a clean wok and stir-fry finely ground ingredients over low heat until fragrant.
- Add remaining ingredients, and bring to a slow boil. Return fried tofu to the wok. Stir and simmer for 2–3 minutes until gravy thickens slightly.
- Serve hot, garnished with coriander leaves.

Spicy Minced Chicken, Tofu and Lady's Fingers

This dish is a contrast of textures and colours. The lady's fingers must be cooked just right so that they retain their colour and crunch.

Ingredients

Chicken meat, preferably thigh	250 g skinned and minced
Light soy sauce	1 Tbsp
Sugar	1 tsp
Sunflower or corn oil	2 Tbsp
Lady's fingers	300 g, cut into 1.5-cm lengths
Fresh chicken stock or water	175 ml (refer to page 18)
Firm tofu	2 pieces, diced small, deep-fried and drained
Red capsicum	$^1/_2$, diced small

Finely Ground

Red chillies	6, seeded
Garlic	4 cloves, peeled
Shallots	6, peeled
Dried prawn paste	2.5-cm square
Light soy sauce	1 Tbsp
Salt	$^1/_4$ tsp

Method

- Season chicken with light soy sauce and sugar and set aside for at least 15 minutes.
- Heat oil in a wok and fry finely ground ingredients over medium heat until fragrant.
- Add seasoned chicken and cook for 1–2 minutes or until chicken changes colour. Add lady's fingers and stir-fry to mix well.
- Add chicken stock or water and bring to a slow boil. Add the tofu and capsicum and simmer for 2–3 minutes until the vegetables are just cooked. Serve hot.

Note: The lady's fingers should only be sliced just before cooking to prevent them from going gluey or sappy.

Spinach and Fermented Soy Bean Cake Curry

A not-too-spicy curry that is vibrantly coloured with the use of turmeric, this dish also contains all the nutritious goodness of spinach and the earthy flavoured fermented soy bean cake.

Ingredients

Sunflower or corn oil	1 Tbsp
Onion	1 small, peeled, halved and sliced
Garlic	2 cloves, peeled and sliced
Coconut milk	500 ml, extracted from 175 g grated coconut and 500 ml water
Salt	1$\frac{1}{2}$ tsp
Fermented soy bean cake	350 g, cut into 2.5-cm cubes
Spinach	200 g

Finely Ground

Red chillies	3, seeded
Garlic	4 cloves, peeled
Ginger	2.5-cm knob, peeled
Turmeric	4-cm knob, peeled
Palm sugar	1 Tbsp, chopped

Garnish

Crisp-fried shallots

Method

- Heat oil in a deep saucepan and fry onion and garlic for a minute.
- Add finely ground ingredients and fry over medium low heat until fragrant.
- Add coconut milk and bring to the boil. Add salt, fermented soy bean cake and spinach.
- Stir and simmer uncovered until vegetables soften and gravy thickens a little.
- Garnish with crisp-fried shallots and serve.

Steamed Chicken, Tofu Otak-otak with Lemon Basil

A quick dish that adds spice to white rice, and is also delicious as a sandwich filling.

Ingredients

Chicken thigh meat	400 g, skinned and cut into 1.5-cm cubes
Salt	1^1/$_2$ tsp
Sugar	1 tsp
White pepper	^{1}/$_4$ tsp
Shallots	6, peeled and sliced
Red chillies	3, sliced
Bird's eyes chillies	3, sliced
Spring onions	3, sliced
Lemon basil leaves	30 g
Large eggs	2, beaten
Semi-soft tofu	1 piece, diced small and lightly fried
Fresh coconut cream	2 Tbsp (refer to page 119)
Salam leaves	5
Lemon grass	3 stalks , bruised

Finely Ground

Candlenuts	6
Garlic	3 cloves, peeled
Turmeric	3-cm knob, peeled
Ginger	3-cm knob, peeled
Galangal	3-cm knob, peeled
Lemon grass	2 stalks, sliced

Method

- Season chicken with salt, sugar and pepper and set aside for 30 minutes.
- Combine chicken with finely ground ingredients, sliced shallots, chillies, spring onions, basil leaves and beaten egg. Add tofu and coconut cream and mix well.
- Line base of a round 19-cm diameter and 8-cm deep heat-proof dish with *salam* leaves. Place lemon grass on top. Pour in combined mixture.
- Steam over rapidly boiling water for 20 minutes. Transfer to serving dish and serve hot.

Tofu and Eggs in Spicy Soy Sauce

A simple dish of tofu and egg in gravy flavoured with fragrant tangy spices and aromatic onions and lemon grass.

Ingredients

Semi-soft tofu	3 pieces
Oil for deep-frying	
Hard-boiled eggs	7, shelled and halved
Sunflower or corn oil	1 Tbsp
Cloves	2
Star anise	2 segments
Cinnamon stick	2-cm long
Onion	1, peeled, halved and sliced
Lemon grass	2 stalks, bruised
Tomato sambal	2 Tbsp (refer to page 126)
Fresh chicken stock	350 ml (refer to page 18)
Light soy sauce	2 Tbsp
Thick soy sauce	2 Tbsp
Indonesian sweet soy sauce	2 Tbsp
Lime juice	1 Tbsp
Red chilli	1, seeded and sliced

Method

- Deep-fry the tofu in hot oil until golden. Drain and cut each into 8 portions. Place tofu in the centre of a serving dish and arrange hard boiled eggs around the tofu.
- To make the gravy: heat sunflower or corn oil in a saucepan and fry the spices until aromatic. Add the onions and lemon grass and stir-fry until onions are soft. Stir in the tomato sambal. Add chicken stock, light soy sauce, thick soy sauce and sweet soy sauce. Stir gently and bring to the boil. Reduce heat and simmer for 20 minutes. Stir in lime juice and chilli.
- Pour gravy over the tofu and eggs and serve.

Stir-fried Masala Potato and Tofu

This simple recipe is a real treat for lovers of spicy potatoes. Serve as a main meal accompanied with chapati, naan or puri.

Ingredients

Potatoes	300 g, peeled and cut into 1.5-cm cubes
Firm tofu	1 piece, cut into 1.5-cm cubes
Oil for deep-frying	
Sunflower or corn oil	2 Tbsp
Fenugreek seeds	$1/4$ tsp
Dried chillies	2, rinsed and each cut into 2
Turmeric powder	$1/2$ tsp
Onions	2 medium, peeled and diced
Young ginger	2-cm knob, peeled and finely chopped
Chilli powder	$1/2$ tsp
Garam masala	1 tsp
Light soy sauce	1 Tbsp
Salt	$1/2$ tsp
Fresh chicken stock or water	3 Tbsp (refer to page 18)
Green chilli	1, chopped

Method

- Soak the diced potatoes in a little salt water to prevent discolouration. Drain.
- Drain tofu in a colander.
- Heat oil in a wok and deep-fry the potatoes until light golden and just cooked. Drain and set aside.
- Reheat the oil and deep-fry the tofu until lightly golden. Drain and set aside.
- Heat the sunflower or corn oil in a clean wok. Add the fenugreek seeds, dried chillies and turmeric powder and stir-fry for a few seconds. Add onion and cook for 1 minute. Add ginger, chilli powder and garam masala. Stir well.
- Return the potatoes to the wok and fry for 2 minutes. Add the tofu and toss to mix well.
- Add soy sauce, salt and fresh chicken stock or water. Lastly stir in the green chillies. Serve hot.

Rice & Noodles

Fried Olive Rice with Tofu

This unique and fragrant rice dish is popular in Kuching, Sarawak, where Chinese black olives are easily available. An equally tasty version can be made without dried prawns and chicken, but with an extra half teaspoonful of salt.

Ingredients

Sunflower or corn oil	2 Tbsp
Shallots	2, peeled and sliced
Garlic	3 cloves, peeled and minced
Large eggs	2, lightly beaten with a pinch of salt and a pinch of white pepper
Chinese black olives	90 g seeded, coarsely chopped
Red chillies	2, seeded and chopped
Dried prawns	1 Tbsp, finely ground and toasted
Chicken	75 g, shredded, mixed with a pinch of salt and a pinch of white pepper
Rice	600 g, cooked
Salt	$1/2$ tsp
Sugar	$1/2$ tsp
Mixed frozen vegetables	125 g
Red capsicum	1 small, diced
Firm tofu	2 pieces, cut into small cubes

Garnish

Crisp-fried shallots	1 Tbsp
Spring onions	2, chopped

Method

- Heat 1 Tbsp oil in a wok and lightly brown shallots and garlic. Push the fried ingredients to the side of the wok. Add remaining oil and pour in beaten eggs. Stir-fry the eggs, breaking them into small pieces until cooked and set. Remove the eggs to a dish and set aside.
- Bring the fried shallots and garlic back to the centre of the wok and add black olives and chillies. Stir for 1 minute or until fragrant. Add the dried prawns and chicken and cook for another minute.
- Add cooked rice, breaking up lumps if any. Add salt and sugar. Stir well and cook over high heat for 2–3 minutes.
- Add the mixed vegetables, capsicum and tofu and stir-fry to mix thoroughly. Finally, return eggs to the wok.
- Serve, garnished with crisp-fried shallot and spring onions.

Tofu, Almond and Raisin Rice

A delicious and complete meal in itself, this dish is lightened by the fresh flavour of herbs and raisins.

Ingredients

Butter	70 g
Sunflower oil	60 ml
Onions	2 medium, peeled and chopped
Salam leaves	2 stalks, bruised
Lemon grass	4
Almonds	175 g, blanched
Firm tofu	175 g blanched and diced
Basmati rice	450 g, rinsed and drained
Lemon rind	grated from 1 lemon
Chicken stock	720 ml (refer to page 18)
Chicken stock granules	2 tsp
Salt	1 tsp
Golden raisins	85 g
Coriander leaves	1 Tbsp, chopped
Spring onions	1 Tbsp, chopped
Mint leaves	30 g, chopped
Lemon juice	1 Tbsp

Method

- Heat butter and sunflower oil in a deep non-stick saucepan and stir-fry onions, lemon grass and *salam* leaves until fragrant. Add almonds and tofu and mix well.
- Add the rice and lemon rind and fry for a minute. Add the chicken stock and stock granules. Stir well and add salt, raisins, coriander leaves and spring onions.
- Add mint leaves and lastly the lemon juice. Stir well. Cover the saucepan and bring to the boil. Reduce heat and simmer for 5 minutes.
- Transfer contents to a heat-proof casserole pot. Cover the pot.
- Bake in a preheated oven (fan-assisted) at 175°C for 25–30 minutes or until rice is cooked through. Serve hot.

Fried Rice Indonesian Style

This colourful rice dish is another complete meal in itself although fried rice is often served together with many other dishes. The fried baby anchovies add flavour and a crisp crunch to the rice.

Ingredients

Sunflower or corn oil	2 Tbsp
Shallots	2, peeled and sliced
Spicy prawn paste (sambal belacan)*	2 Tbsp
Eggs	2
Frozen mixed vegetables	150 g
Firm tofu	2 pieces, diced and fried
Cooked rice	550 g
Salt	$1/2$ tsp
Sugar	1 tsp
White pepper	$1/4$ tsp
Baby anchovies	40 g, fried

Method

- Heat a wok or large frying pan and add the oil. Add the shallots and spicy prawn paste and stir-fry over medium heat until aromatic.
- Break the eggs into the wok and stir to mix and break up the cooked eggs. Add the mixed vegetables and tofu and toss for 1–2 minutes.
- Add the cooked rice, salt, sugar, pepper and fried baby anchovies, stirring to mix well over high heat. Serve hot.

Note: When rice is fried with spicy prawn paste (sambal belacan), it becomes distinctly and pleasantly aromatic.

*Spicy Prawn Paste

Ingredients

Dried prawn paste	5-cm piece or 2 Tbsp dried prawn paste granules
Red chillies	8

Method

- Roast the dried prawn paste or the granules in a dry pan over low heat until aromatic.
- Put the roasted prawn paste and the chillies in a mini food processor and blend until smooth.
- Use as required or freeze for later use.

Note: The secret of good spicy prawn paste is using good grade dried prawn paste. My favourite prawn paste is from a small town called Bintulu in Sarawak. The paste is made from 100 percent baby prawns (udang geragau) with no preservatives added. These baby prawns invade the Bintulu coastal areas in March and September and the local people will begin their hard work, wading deep into the sea while pushing a net in front of them to scoop up the small prawns. The locals make enough prawn paste for their own consumption and a little extra for sale in their own markets.

Kashmiri Chicken Pulao with Tofu

A vegetable curry dish, such as dhal or potato and pea curry, complements this dish beautifully.

Chicken

Chicken thighs	4 (whole), skinned
Salt	1 tsp
White pepper	$1/4$ tsp
Sunflower or corn oil	1 Tbsp
Onion	1 small, peeled and chopped
Cloves	2
Bay leaves	3
Black peppercorns	12

Rice

Basmati rice	450 g
Ghee	2 Tbsp
Onions	2, peeled and sliced
Whole almonds	20, blanched and toasted
Green cardamoms	4, podded
Garlic	5 cloves, peeled and ground
Ginger	2.5-cm knob, peeled and ground
Black peppercorns	8
Cloves	4
Poppy seeds	1 tsp, ground
Cinnamon stick	2.5-cm
Cumin powder	1 tsp
Garam masala	1 tsp
Yoghurt	150 ml
Coriander	2 Tbsp, chopped
Mint (optional)	2 Tbsp, chopped
Water	700 ml
Salt	2 tsp
Firm tofu	1 piece, diced and fried

Garnish

Crisp-fried shallots	
Almond flakes	50 g, blanched and toasted

Method for Cooking Chicken

- Season chicken with salt and pepper.
- Heat oil and fry the onions until soft. Add cloves, bay leaves and peppercorn and stir until aromatic. Add chicken and cook until chicken changes colour. Sprinkle in a little water if necessary.
- Remove chicken when half-cooked. Set aside.

Method for Cooking Rice

- Wash the rice and drain well. Heat ghee and lightly brown onions. Add almonds, cardamoms, garlic and ginger and cook for 1 minute. Add remaining spices and stir for another minute. Add yoghurt and mix well. Add chopped coriander and mint leaves.
- Transfer rice mixture to an electric rice cooker. Add water, salt and tofu and mix well. Top with chicken. Cook until rice is done.
- Serve garnished with crisp-fried shallots and almonds.

Thai Laksa

A popular Thai noodle dish, this can be eaten as a light meal anytime.

Gravy Ingredients

Chubb mackerel	3 kg, cleaned
Salt	2 tsp
Sunflower or corn oil	60 ml
Dried anchovies	250 g, cleaned, rinsed and drained
Water	1 1/2 litres
Torch ginger bud	2–3 stalks (outer petals removed), stems and inner buds finely sliced
Tamarind juice	2 Tbsp tamarind pulp, mixed with 250 ml water and strained
Fish sauce	1 Tbsp
Coconuts	3, grated and squeezed to extract 500 ml thick coconut milk and add 2 1/4 litres water for thin coconut milk
Fried tofu puffs (round)	15 pieces, scalded and halved
Sweet basil leaves	10–12 stalks

Finely Ground A

Dried chillies	30, soaked to soften
Fresh red chillies	8
Turmeric	1-cm knob

Finely Ground B

Shallots	30–35, peeled
Garlic	1 head, peeled
Candlenuts	10
Lemon grass	10 stalks, outer hard portions removed and reserved for anchovy stock

Laksa Ingredients

Fresh laksa noodles	2 kg, scalded and drained
Sunflower or corn oil	2 Tbsp
Bean sprouts	600 g, tailed and scalded

Garnish

Cucumbers	2, peeled and shredded
Mint	1–2 bunches

Method

- Rub fish with salt and steam over rapidly boiling water for 10 minutes. When cool enough to handle, debone the fish.
- Heat 2 Tbsp sunflower or corn oil and fry anchovies for 3 minutes. Add water, outer petals and stems of torch ginger bud. Add the outer hard portions of lemon grass. Bring to a boil, reduce heat and simmer for 30 minutes. Strain the stock and set aside.
- Heat remaining oil and fry finely ground ingredients A for 3 minutes. Add finely ground ingredients B and stir-fry for 8 minutes until fragrant.
- Pour in the stock and tamarind juice. Add fish sauce and bring to the boil. Add thin coconut milk and tofu. When stock reboils, add basil leaves. Simmer for 5–10 minutes. Then add fish meat and thick coconut milk. Add salt to taste.
- To serve, add sunflower or corn oil to noodles, stir well, and put a handful of noodles and some bean sprouts into serving bowls. Ladle hot fish gravy over noodles, garnish with cucumber and mint and serve.

Fruity Saffron Pulao

This is a rice dish laced with everything nice: tofu adds a meaty and nutritious bite, saffron and spices perfume the rice, raisins and apricots lend sweetness to carry this meatless rice dish to gastronomic heights.

Ingredients

Saffron strands	$^1/_2$ tsp
Boiling water	1 Tbsp
Basmati rice	250 g
Butter	30 g, at room temperature, combined with 1 Tbsp sunflower oil
Almond flakes	30 g
Walnuts	8, coarsely chopped
Golden raisins	50 g
Dried ready-to-eat apricots	5, diced
Chicken stock granules	10 g, mixed with 700 ml water and $^1/_2$ tsp salt
Frozen peas	150 g, scalded for 2 minutes in salted water
Spring onions	2, chopped
Coriander leaves	2 Tbsp, chopped
Firm tofu	3 pieces, diced small and fried

Spices

Cloves	4
Cardamoms	2, podded
Cinnamon stick	2.5-cm

Garnish

Red chilli	1, sliced

Method

- Immerse saffron strands in the boiling water to infuse. Set aside for 15 minutes.
- Rinse the rice and drain in a colander.
- In a non-stick wok, heat half the butter and oil mixture and stir-fry the almonds and walnuts for a few seconds. Add the raisins and apricots and toss until the raisins are lightly browned and plumped up. Dish out and set aside.
- Reheat wok. Add the remaining butter and oil mixture and fry the spices until aromatic. Add the rice and mix well for 1 minute. Add the saffron water and chicken stock mixture. Bring to the boil. Cover, reduce heat and simmer for 10 minutes.
- Transfer rice to a heat-proof dish or pot and bake in preheated oven (fan-assisted or conventional) at 175ºC for 15 minutes. Add peas, spring onions and coriander leaves, and stir. Cover the pot and continue to bake for a further 10–15 minutes or until rice is done.
- Sprinkle fried tofu over the rice and garnish with red chilli.

Note: Serve with any vegetable, meat or seafood curry for a delightful evening meal. Just before serving, fluff up the rice lightly with a pair of chopsticks.

Rainbow Vegetable Pulao

A blend of saffron, rose water and spice delicately perfume and colour the rice. It may take a while to prepare the dish but it is well worth the time as the rice dish can be served as a complete meal in itself.

Ingredients

Saffron strands	1 tsp
Boiling water	250 ml
Ghee	1 Tbsp
Sunflower or corn oil	1 Tbsp
Cardamoms	2, podded
Cinnamon stick	2-cm length
Cloves	2
Onion	$1/2$, peeled and chopped
Garlic	2 cloves, peeled chopped
Ginger	1 tsp chopped, peeled
Basmati rice	450 g, soaked for 30 minutes and drained
Coriander powder	1 tsp
Cumin seeds	1 tsp
Chilli powder	$1/4$ tsp
Ground almonds	1 Tbsp
Water	525 ml
Chicken stock	1 cube
Salt	1 tsp
Rose water	1 tsp
Yellow food colouring	$1/2$ tsp
Green food colouring	$1/4$ tsp
Cooked vegetables*	

Garnish
Crisp-fried shallots
Roasted almond flakes

Method
- Immerse saffron strands in boiling water and set aside for at least 30 minutes.
- Heat the ghee and sunflower or corn oil and fry cardamoms, cinnamon and cloves. Add onion, garlic and ginger and fry until fragrant.
- Add rice, coriander, cumin and chilli powder and toss until rice is coated with ghee and spices. Add ground almonds and mix well.
- Transfer to a rice cooker and add saffron water. Stir well. Add water, chicken stock and salt. Mix thoroughly and cook until rice is done.
- When rice is cooked, stir the rose water into the rice. Divide the rice into 3 portions. Colour 1 portion yellow and 1 portion green. Leave the third portion uncoloured.
- Fill a rectangular casserole dish with alternate layers of rice and cooked vegetables in the following order: green rice, half the vegetables, uncoloured rice, remaining vegetables and finally the yellow rice. Sprinkle some shallot crisps and roasted almond flakes over each layer of rice.
- Put the dish in a preheated oven to bake at 50°C for 30 minutes.

*Cooked Vegetables

Ingredients

Ghee	1 Tbsp
Sunflower or corn oil	1 Tbsp
Cinnamon	2-cm stick
Cardamom	1, podded
Clove	1
Cumin seeds	1 tsp
Garlic	3 cloves, peeled and chopped
Ginger	1 tsp chopped and peeled
Carrots	100 g, peeled and diced
French beans	120 g, cut into 0.5-cm lengths
Tomatoes	2 medium, diced
Firm tofu	1 piece, diced and deep-fried
Red chillies	2, diced
Green chilli	1, diced
Red or green capsicum	1, diced
Yoghurt	2 Tbsp
Tomato sauce	1 Tbsp
Salt	1 tsp

Method
- Heat ghee and sunflower or corn oil and fry spices, garlic and ginger. Add the carrots, French beans, tomatoes and tofu. Stir well and add chillies and capsicum.
- Stir in yoghurt, tomato sauce and salt and simmer for 3–5 minutes. Dish out and use as required.

Fried Rice with Mushrooms and Pine Nuts

Fried rice lends itself to many variations and everyone has a favourite version. This is mine. The cloud-ear fungus and mushrooms give an enjoyable chewy, crunchy texture and the soft oily pine nuts a wonderful delicate aroma.

Ingredients

Sunflower oil	2 Tbsp
Pine nuts	40 g
Shallots	2, peeled and sliced
Young ginger	1 Tbsp, chopped and peeled
Fresh cloud-ear fungus	5, shredded
Fresh Shiitake mushrooms	3, diced small
Frozen mixed vegetables	125 g
Firm tofu	1 piece, diced small and fried
Cold cooked rice	550 g

Sauce

Light soy sauce	2 Tbsp
Thick soy sauce	1 tsp
Sugar	1 tsp
Salt	$1/2$ tsp

Method

- Heat sunflower oil in a wok and stir-fry the pine nuts for a few seconds until they are light golden. Remove from the oil and set aside.
- Add the shallots and the ginger to wok and fry until lightly browned and aromatic. Add cloud-ear fungus and mushrooms and fry for a minute. Add the mixed vegetables and stir-fry for 1–2 minutes. Add the tofu and rice, stirring to mix well.
- Combine sauce ingredients and add to wok. Toss rice for 3 minutes. Add the pine nuts and mix well. Serve hot.

Note: The high oil content in pine nuts makes them burn easily when roasted or fried in oil. Fry over medium-low heat and watch them like a hawk. As soon as they begin to turn light golden, remove quickly with a perforated ladle. They will continue to brown after being taken out of the frying pan.

Lontong

Lontong is a rice cake and vegetable curry dish which can be eaten as a complete meal. The rice cake is made by compressing boiled rice into slabs which are then cut into cubes. Known as ketupat, the rice is also sold in supermarkets.

Ingredients

Ketupat rice	1 packet (130 g), boiled according to instructions on pack and cubed
Sunflower or corn oil	2 Tbsp
Lemon grass	3 stalks, smashed
Galangal	5-cm knob, peeled and smashed
Dried prawns	35 g, rinsed, finely blended and toasted
Anchovy stock	1$^1/_2$ litres (refer to page 113)
Salt	1 tsp or to taste
Chinese turnip	200 g, cut into 1 x 5-cm fingers
Long beans	75 g, cut into 5-cm lengths
Cabbage	100 g, cut into 5-cm squares
Dried bean curd sticks	50 g, soaked to soften and cut into 5-cm lengths
Pre-fried soft tofu	15 pieces
Firm tofu	2 pieces, fried and cut into cubes
Transparent noodles	50 g, soaked to soften and scalded
Coconut cream	250 ml , extracted from 350 g grated coconut

Finely Ground

Red chillies	3, seeded
Shallots	10, peeled
Garlic	4 cloves, peeled
Turmeric	20 g, peeled
Young galangal	2.5-cm knob, peeled

Method

- Heat oil and fry finely ground ingredients together with lemon grass and galangal over low heat for about 5–8 minutes or until fragrant.
- Add dried prawns and fry for 1–2 minutes. Add anchovy stock and stir in salt. When stock begins to boil, add all the vegetables and tofu and cook for 5 minutes. Add transparent noodles and coconut milk. Stir. When the curry boils, remove from heat.
- To serve, put a few rice cubes into a bowl and top with the vegetable curry.

Note: To toast blended dried prawns, pan-fry in a dry wok over medium heat until dry and aromatic.

Saffron Rice with Mushrooms and Tomatoes

This is another deliciously aromatic one-dish meal. For a different flavour, dice 150 g smoked salami, bacon or turkey and add to the rice.

Ingredients

Saffron strands	$1/2$ tsp
Boiling water	85 ml
Long-grain rice	450 g, washed and drained
Fresh chicken stock	610 ml (refer to page 18)
Sunflower or corn oil	60 ml
Shallots	4, peeled sliced
Garlic	3 cloves, peeled chopped
Young ginger	3-cm knob, peeled and chopped
Cinnamon	5-cm stick
Cardamoms	6, podded
Black peppercorns	$1/2$ tsp
Bay leaves	2
Oyster or button mushrooms	100 g, diced into 1-cm pieces
Firm tofu	2 pieces, diced small and deep-fried
Salt	2 tsp
White pepper	$1/2$ tsp
Sugar	1 tsp
Cherry tomatoes	18, quartered
Coriander leaves	2 Tbsp, chopped
Parsley	2 Tbsp, chopped
Spring onions	1 Tbsp, chopped
Cashew nuts	90 g (roasted) or 45 g roasted almond flakes

Garnish
Sweet basil

Method

- Immerse saffron strands in boiling water and leave to infuse for 15 minutes.
- Cook rice with saffron mixture and chicken stock in a rice cooker. When the rice is cooked, set aside to cool. Loosen grains with a pair of chopsticks.
- Heat oil in a large non-stick wok and lightly brown shallot, garlic and ginger.
- Add spices and bay leaves. Stir for a few seconds, then add the mushrooms. When the mushrooms are almost cooked, add fried tofu and season with salt, pepper and sugar. Mix thoroughly.
- Add the cooked rice and toss well. Add cherry tomatoes and stir-fry until tomatoes are hot but still hold their shape.
- Stir in all the fresh herbs and lastly the cashew nuts or almond flakes.
- Garnish with fresh sweet basil and serve.

Note: If you must wash the oyster mushrooms, rinse quickly and squeeze out any excess water.

Tomato, Chicken and Almond Tofu Rice

The enticing aroma of herbs and spices adds to the appeal of this tomato-flavoured rice dish.

Ingredients

Butter	35 g
Olive oil or sunflower oil	3 Tbsp
Almonds	75 g, blanched
Firm tofu	1 piece, diced small
Onions	3, peeled and coarsely chopped
Garlic	5 cloves, peeled and coarsely chopped
Cinnamon	3-cm stick
Cardamoms	6, podded
Bay leaves	3
Basmati rice	900 g, washed and rinsed
Tomato puree	2 Tbsp
Whole tomatoes	1 can, (about 400 g), peeled and chopped finely
Fresh chicken stock or water	1 litre (refer to page 18)
Chicken stock granules	2 tsp
Coriander leaves	3 Tbsp, chopped
Dark raisins	50 g

Marinate for 30 Minutes

Chicken thighs	2, skinned and chopped into bite-sized pieces
Salt	1 tsp
Ground black pepper	1 tsp
Allspice	1 tsp
Paprika	2 tsp
Cinnamon powder	$1/2$ tsp

Method

- Heat butter and olive or sunflower oil and stir-fry the almonds for 3–5 minutes. Drain and set aside.
- Fry tofu in the same oil for 2–3 minutes. Drain and set aside.
- Stir-fry marinated chicken for 5 minutes or until half-cooked. Remove and set aside.
- Stir-fry onions and garlic for about 3 minutes. Add spices and bay leaves and sauté until onion is lightly golden. Add rice and toss well.
- Stir in tomato purée and chopped tomato together with its juice from the can. Pour in the chicken stock and granules. Bring to the boil. Add the half-cooked chicken and cook over low heat for 10–15 minutes. Add coriander leaves and raisins. Stir well.
- Transfer to a heat-proof casserole dish. Cover and bake in a pre-heated oven (fan-assisted or conventional) at 175°C for 30–40 minutes or until rice is cooked through. Sprinkle fried almonds and tofu over rice and serve hot.

Waxed Duck Rice

The best part of making this dish is when you lift the lid of the rice pot and the delicious aroma wafts up. This is a dish that calls for second helpings.

Ingredients

Rice	450 g, washed and drained
Water	570 ml
Waxed salted duck thigh	1
Waxed sweet duck meat	1
Chinese sausages	2
Arrowhead	4, peeled and thickly sliced

Gravy

Fresh chicken stock	125 ml (refer to page 18)
Oyster sauce	1 tsp
Light soy sauce	1 Tbsp
Sugar	1 tsp
Thick soy sauce	1/2 tsp
Sesame oil	1/4 tsp

Garnish

Dried sweet bean curd	2 pieces, rinsed, shredded and fried
Spring onions	1, chopped
Coriander leaves	1 sprig, chopped

Method

- Boil rice and water in an electric rice cooker for approximately 10 minutes.
- Scald the waxed salted duck, the sweet duck meat and sausages in a saucepan of boiling water for 2–3 minutes.
- Drain and slice off the skins and as much of the fats as you wish. Do not remove too much fat as the fragrance of the rice depends on the fat and the juices of the meat infusing the rice with their sweet flavours. Remove the skins of the sausages.
- Chop the waxed salted duck into 1-cm pieces and slice the sweet duck meat.
- Slice the sausages diagonally, 0.5-cm thick. When the rice comes to the boil, spread and press the arrow head into the rice. Top with the meat and sausages. Cover the rice cooker and cook until rice is done.
- Just before serving the rice, transfer meat and sausages to a serving dish and set aside. Stir and fluff up the rice with a pair of chopsticks to distribute the oil evenly. Do this gently to prevent the arrowhead from breaking up. Return the meat to the pot and stir to mix evenly.
- Serve duck rice garnished with sweet bean curd crisps, spring onions, and coriander leaves. Combine sauce ingredients and serve sauce in separate bowl with the rice.

Note: Waxed duck meat and Chinese sausages are readily available before the Chinese New Year.

These delicacies from China are prepared soon after the mid-autumn or Mooncake Festival when the north winds (essential for drying and curing waxed meat and sausages) blow in the wintry months of China. The best waxed ducks come from Nan An in Fujian province, southern China, where the ducks feed in ponds teeming with prawns.

Arrowheads are slightly larger than water chestnuts. The outer skin is cream coloured. They are also imported from China and are readily available during the Chinese New Year. Besides being braised or stir-fried, arrowheads can be made into chips.

Fried Loh Shee Fun

This stir-fried noodle dish is great when you have to cook up a meal at short notice for family or friends.

Ingredients

Fresh short round rice noodles	600 g
Sunflower or corn oil	1 Tbsp
Shallots	3, peeled and sliced
Garlic	3 cloves, peeled and finely minced
Dried Chinese mushrooms	3, diced
Chicken thigh (whole)	1, skinned, diced and seasoned with a little salt and ground white pepper
Turkey bacon (ham)	75 g (preferably smoked), diced
Thick mustard green stems	3–4, cut into 0.5-cm thickness
Chinese rice wine	1 Tbsp
Pre-fried tofu	8 pieces, diced
Bean sprouts	200 g, rinsed and tailed
Fresh chicken stock	3 Tbsp (refer to page 18)

Garnish

Crisp-fried shallots	2 Tbsp
Spring onions	2, chopped
Coriander leaves	2 sprigs, chopped

Sauce

Light soy sauce	1 Tbsp
Thick soy sauce	1 Tbsp
Black sweet soy sauce	1 Tbsp
Sugar	$1/2$ tsp
Salt	$1/2$ tsp
White pepper	$1/4$ tsp

Method

- Add a little sunflower or corn oil to a pot of boiling water and scald rice noodles for 1 minute.
- Heat 1 Tbsp sunflower or corn oil in a wok and lightly brown shallots and garlic.
- Add mushrooms and chicken and stir-fry briskly. When the chicken changes colour, add turkey bacon (ham) and toss for a few seconds. Add mustard greens and Chinese rice wine. Add tofu and bean sprouts and toss briefly.
- Add the sauce and, finally, the scalded noodles. Continue to stir-fry for 2–3 minutes. Stir in chicken stock and fry until the liquid evaporates.
- Remove to a serving dish and sprinkle with crisp-fried shallots, spring onions and coriander leaves.

Fried Rice Vermicelli with Tofu and Water Chestnuts

Another quick, easy dish that is ideal for a light snack or brunch.

Ingredients

Sunflower or corn oil	2 Tbsp
Garlic	6 cloves, peeled and finely chopped
Ginger	4 thick slices, peeled and finely chopped
Shallots	3, peeled and sliced
Spring onions	6, cut into 3-cm lengths and separate white and green parts
Hot garlic bean paste or preserved soy bean paste	1 Tbsp
Chilli bean paste	1 Tbsp
Red chillies	4, finely shredded
Bean sprouts	225 g, rinsed and tailed
Fresh water chestnuts	10, peeled and finely shredded
Firm tofu	1 piece, shredded
Rice vermicelli	250 g, soaked in water for 20–30 minutes and drained

Sauce

Light soy sauce	2 Tbsp
Thick soy sauce	$^1/_2$ Tbsp
Chinese rice wine	2 Tbsp
Salt	$^1/_2$ tsp
Ground white pepper	$^1/_4$ tsp
Sugar	$^1/_2$ tsp
Fresh chicken stock or mushrooom stock	125 ml (refer to page 18 or 20)

Method

- Heat wok and add oil. When the oil is hot, lightly brown garlic, ginger and shallots. Add the white parts of the spring onion, hot garlic bean paste and chilli bean sauce. Stir well.
- Add chillies, bean sprouts, water chestnuts and tofu and stir-fry for 1 minute. Combine the sauce ingredients and add to wok. Add rice vermicelli. Toss well for 3–5 minutes until well combined.
- Serve garnished with green parts of spring onions.

Char Choo Mee

This is a Foochow home-style noodle dish popular in Sibu, Sarawak. It is easy to cook and can be a delicious part of any meal or a dish served on its own. The secret to this tasty dish is to thoroughly sear the noodles in a hot wok. 'Char Choo Mee' literally means 'Fried and Braised Noodles'.

Ingredients

Chicken	150 g skinned and sliced
Salt	$1^1/_2$ tsp
White pepper	$^1/_4$ tsp
Fresh yellow noodles	500 g
Sunflower or corn oil	2 Tbsp
Shallots	2, peeled and sliced
Garlic	3 cloves, peeled and minced
Fresh chicken stock	700 ml (refer to page 18)
Thick soy sauce	$^1/_2$ tsp
Light soy sauce	1 Tbsp
Medium–large prawns	8, eyes and feelers trimmed
Pre-fried tofu	20 pieces
Mustard greens or baby Chinese chard	150 g
Spring onions	2 Tbsp, chopped

Method

- Season chicken with $^1/_2$ tsp salt and pepper and set aside for 15 minutes.
- Bring a large saucepan of water to the boil and scald the noodles for a few seconds. Drain well and set aside.
- Heat sunflower or corn oil in a wok and lightly brown shallots and garlic. Add noodles and 1 tsp salt and fry over high heat for 3–5 minutes or until the noodles are half-cooked. Pour in chicken stock, add thick and light soy sauces and stir well. When stock begins to boil, add chicken, prawns, tofu and vegetables. Cover the wok and simmer for 5 minutes.
- Remove and serve hot, garnished with spring onions.

Hoisin Noodles

Vegetables are the main ingredient in this simple noodle dish, scented with the fragrance of sesame oil.

Ingredients

Sunflower or corn oil	2 Tbsp
Sesame oil	$1/_2$ Tbsp
Ginger	3 thick slices, peeled and chopped
Garlic	3 cloves, peeled and chopped
Shallots	2, peeled and sliced
Dried Chinese mushrooms	2, soaked to soften and shredded
Cabbage leaves	3, shredded
Sugar snap or mange-tout peas	100 g
Firm tofu	2 pieces, cubed and deep-fried
Thin spaghetti or dried egg noodles	250 g, cooked

Sauce

Fresh chicken stock	3 Tbsp (refer to page 18)
Hoisin sauce	3 Tbsp
Light soy sauce	2 Tbsp
White pepper	$1/_2$ tsp
Salt	$1/_4$ tsp

Garnish

Spring onions	1 Tbsp, chopped
Coriander leaves	1 Tbsp, chopped

Method

- Heat sunflower or corn oil and sesame oil in a wok. Stir-fry ginger, garlic and shallots until lightly browned.
- Add mushrooms and cook for a minute. Add cabbage and stir-fry for 2–3 minutes. Add peas and fried tofu and toss briefly.
- Pour in the sauce. When it begins to boil, add spaghetti or noodles. Toss until well mixed.
- Remove to a serving dish. Serve hot, garnished with chopped spring onions and coriander leaves.

Kerabu Bee Hoon

An unusual noodle dish with a combination of flavours. Sliced raw vegetables add a delightful sharpness.

Ingredients

Firm tofu	2 pieces, shredded
Oil for deep-frying	
Small prawns	300 g shelled, deveined and diced
Cuttlefish	150 g, cut into 2-cm strips
Salt	$1/2$ tsp
White pepper	$1/4$ tsp
Rice vermicelli	300 g
Bean sprouts	300 g, tailed
Dried prawns	150 g, rinsed and ground
Dried prawn paste granules	1 Tbsp, toasted
Red chillies	15, seeded and finely blended

Sauce

Lemon juice	135 ml
Sugar	2 Tbsp
Light soy sauce	2 Tbsp
Fish sauce	3 Tbsp

Sliced

Shallots	12, peeled
Lemon grass	3 stalks, tough outer layers discarded
Bird's eye chillies	15
Torch ginger bud	2, outer leaves discarded
Kaffir lime leaves	6
Sweet basil leaves	20

Garnish

Peanuts	3 Tbsp, toasted and coarsely ground

Method

- Heat oil in a wok. Deep-fry shredded tofu until golden brown. Drain on absorbent kitchen paper. Set aside.
- Season prawns and cuttlefish with salt and pepper.
- Bring a large saucepan of water to the boil. Scald bean sprouts and rice vermicelli separately. Drain and spread them on a bamboo tray or colander.
- In a small saucepan, bring water to the boil. Scald prawns and cuttlefish. Drain well and set aside. Retain stock.
- Heat a wok or saucepan without adding oil and pan roast ground dried prawns until fragrant. Remove and set aside. Toast prawn paste granules in same pan until fragrant. Add to dried prawns.
- Add the freshly blended chillies and stir until mixture boils. Remove and add to dried prawn and prawn paste granules mixture. Add sauce and sliced ingredients. Mix well. Add 4 Tbsp or more of the reserved stock if you prefer the dish to be more moist.
- Add the rice vermicelli, tofu and bean sprouts. Toss and mix well. Place on a serving dish, sprinkle with toasted peanuts and serve.

Indonesian Soto with Transparent Noodles

This noodle dish comes with a rich and spicy broth, flavoured with a variety of aromatic herbs and spices.

Soup Ingredients

Chicken thigh	1 kg, skinned and deboned
Salt	2 tsp
White pepper	$1/2$ tsp
Oil for deep-frying	
Sunflower or corn oil	1 Tbsp
Lemon grass	3 stalks, smashed
Cinnamon stick	4-cm length
Salam leaves	6
Ginger	3-cm knob, smashed
Fresh chicken stock	4 litres (refer to page 18)
Fresh coconut cream	125 ml (refer to page 119)
Salt or to taste	7 tsp

Finely Ground

Shallots	18, peeled
Candlenuts	4
Garlic	6 cloves, peeled
Ginger	3-cm knob, peeled
Turmeric	3-cm knob, peeled

Spices (mixed with a little water)

Coriander powder	2 $1/2$ Tbsp
Cumin powder	1 tsp
Ground white pepper	$1/2$ tsp

Soto Ingredients

Transparent noodles	300 g, soaked and scalded
Bean sprouts	300 g, tailed and scalded
Firm tofu	6 pieces, fried and sliced
Pre-fried tofu (round)	10 pieces, scalded and quartered
Potatoes	4 large, peeled, cubed and deep-fried
Eggs	6 hard-boiled, shelled and quartered
Kalamansi limes	10, halved
Red chillies	3, seeded and sliced
Green chillies	3, seeded and sliced
Crisp-fried shallots	
Spring onions	3, chopped
Chinese celery	6 sprigs, chopped
Tomatoes	2 ripe, diced
Indonesian sweet soy sauce	
Indonesian crackers	deep-fried

Method

- Season chicken with salt and pepper for 15 minutes. Steam over rapidly boiling water for 15 minutes. Drain well. Heat oil and deep-fry chicken. Cool, shred and set aside.
- To prepare the soup, heat sunflower or corn oil in a deep saucepan and fry finely ground ingredients until fragrant. Add lemon grass, cinnamon stick, *salam* leaves and ginger and fry for 2 minutes. Add spice paste and fry for 30 seconds. Pour in chicken stock and bring to the boil. Add coconut cream and simmer for 5 minutes. Add shredded chicken and salt to taste.
- To serve, put a serving of transparent noodles in individual bowls. Add some bean sprouts, tofu, potatoes, eggs, chillies, crisp-fried shallots, spring onions, celery and tomatoes. Drizzle 2 tsp Indonesian sweet soy sauce into each bowl. Fill with the soup and top with a few pieces of fried crackers.

Note: Compressed rice cakes (*ketupat*) can be used in place of transparent vermicelli.

Sarawak Laksa

This is another popular Asian noodle dish that is delicious served on its own, anytime.

Sambal Ingredients

Dried prawns	100 g, rinsed
Water	250 ml
Sago or cider vinegar	2 Tbsp
Thick soy sauce	1 tsp
Salt	1 tsp
Sugar	2 tsp

Finely Ground

Sunflower or corn oil	60 ml
Dried chillies	25, seeded and soaked to soften
Shallots	300 g, peeled
Garlic	6 cloves, peeled
Dried prawn paste	5-cm piece
Coriander sprouts	2 small bunches
Coriander stems and roots	2 Tbsp, chopped
Coriander powder	1 Tbsp
Ground black pepper	$1/2$ tsp

Gravy Ingredients

Sunflower or corn oil	3 Tbsp
Dried chillies	20, seeded and soaked to soften
Red chillies	3, seeded
Onions	4, peeled and diced
Lemon grass	3 stalks, sliced
Galangal	3-cm knob, peeled
Water or anchovy stock	3 litres (refer to page 113)
Fresh coconut cream	350 ml (refer to page 119)
Sago or cider vinegar	2 Tbsp
Salt	7 tsp
Anchovy stock granules	2 tsp

Laksa Ingredients

Medium prawns	300 g, cleaned and seasoned with $1/4$ tsp each of salt, sugar and ground black pepper
Bean sprouts	500 g, tailed and scalded
Rice vermicelli (medium strand)	600 g, scalded
Fish cakes	3 pieces, scalded, fried and sliced
Pre-fried tofu	6 pieces, scalded and sliced
Eggs	3, fried into thin omelettes and finely shredded
Mini coriander sprouts	3 bunches
Coriander leaves	1 sprig, chopped
Kalamansi limes	12, halved

To Prepare the Sambal

- Blend dried prawns in a food processor or pepper grinder until fine and then fry in an ungreased pan until fragrant. Remove and set aside.
- In the same pan, pour in the finely ground ingredients and fry over medium heat for about 2 minutes until fragrant.
- Add water, vinegar, salt and sugar. Bring to the boil and simmer for 1–2 minutes. Set aside.

To Prepare the Gravy

- Blend sunflower or corn oil, chillies, onions, lemon grass and galangal in an electric blender until fine.
- Transfer to a large saucepan and fry until fragrant, about 10–12 minutes. Add water or anchovy stock and bring to the boil. Add coconut cream, vinegar, salt, anchovy stock granules and seasoned prawns. Simmer for about 5 minutes.

To Serve

- Put 1 Tbsp bean sprouts and a handful of rice vermicelli in a bowl. Top with fish cakes, fried tofu, omelette strips, coriander and half a lime.
- Pour enough hot gravy to cover vermicelli. Top with 1–2 Tbsp sambal and serve.

Indonesian Laksa

The lovely aroma of this one-dish meal comes from the fresh lemon grass, galangal and kaffir lime leaves.

Ingredients

Chicken (whole)	1, 1.5 kg, skinned and halved
Salt	1$^1/_2$ tsp
White pepper	1$^1/_4$ tsp
Small-medium prawns	300 g , shelled and deveined
Sunflower or oil	2 Tbsp
Dried prawns	4 Tbsp, rinsed and finely ground
Galangal	6-cm knob, crushed
Lemon grass	4 stalks, smashed
Salam leaves	6
Kaffir lime leaves	8–10
Low-fat milk	1 litre
Fresh chicken stock	1 litre (refer to page 18)
Fresh coconut cream	2–3 Tbsp (refer to page 119)
Salt	1 Tbsp, or to taste
Crisp-fried shallots	3 Tbsp, crushed
Fine rice vermicelli	800 g, soaked and scalded
Crisp-fried shallots	
Spring onions	3-4, chopped
Indonesian sweet soy sauce	
Kalamansi limes	10, halved

Finely Ground

Onion	300 g large, peeled
Turmeric	1-cm knob, peeled
Garlic	10 cloves, peeled
Dried prawn paste granules	3 tsp
Candlenuts	12
Ginger	6-cm knob, peeled
Lesser galangal	3-cm knob
Coriander powder	2 Tbsp

Garnish

Bean sprouts	300 g, tailed and scalded
Pre-fried tofu (round)	10 pieces, scalded and halved
Firm tofu	8 pieces, fried and sliced
Eggs	4 hard-boiled, shelled and quartered
Red chillies	3, sliced
Green chillies	3, sliced
Bird's eye chillies	10, sliced

Method

- Season chicken with 1 tsp salt and 1 tsp pepper, and steam in a heatproof dish over rapidly boiling water for 15–20 minutes.
- Cool and shred the meat. Set aside.
- Season prawns with remaining salt and pepper and set aside.
- Fry dried prawns in a dry wok until fragrant. Set aside.
- Heat oil in a large saucepan and fry finely ground ingredients over low heat until fragrant. Add dried prawns, galangal, lemon grass, and salam and kaffir lime leaves. Stir well and add low-fat milk and chicken stock. Bring to the boil and simmer for 15 minutes.
- Add prawns, coconut cream, salt and crisp-fried shallots.
- For one serving, place a handful of vermicelli in a bowl. Add garnish. Top with enough gravy and sprinkle with crisp-fried shallots, spring onions, 1 tsp Indonesian sweet soy sauce and half a kalamansi.

Laksa Johor

There are many variations of laksa in Asia. The dried sour fruit overtones in this version imparts an unusual taste. Spaghetti can be used in place of laksa noodles.

Ingredients

Anchovy stock	3 1/2 litres (refer to page 113)
Meat curry powder	10 level Tbsp
Lemon grass	1 stalk, bruised
Polygonum leaves	12 stalks
Torch ginger buds	2, split
Dried sour fruit	3 pieces
Dried prawns	3 Tbsp, rinsed and finely ground
Dried anchovies	45 g, fried and finely ground
Grated coconut	3 Tbsp, dry-fried until golden brown and pounded until oily (kerisik)
Mackerel	6 slices, steamed and flaked
Thick coconut milk	500 ml, extracted from 850 g grated coconut and 500 ml water
Salt	3 tsp or to taste
Fresh laksa noodles	1 1/2 kg, scalded

Finely Ground

Shallots	15, peeled
Onions	2, peeled
Garlic	6 cloves, peeled
Galangal	2.5-cm knob, peeled
Ginger	3-cm knob, peeled
Lemon grass	2 stalks, sliced
Dried prawn paste	5-cm piece

Garnish

Long beans	10–12, cut into 2.5-cm lengths and boiled
Onions	3, peeled and finely sliced
Cucumber	1, shredded
Torch ginger bud	1, sliced
Bean sprouts	300 g, tailed and scalded
Kalamansi limes	8–10, halved
Preserved radish	2 Tbsp chopped, rinsed and pan-fried without oil
Pre-fried soft tofu	20 pieces

Method

- Bring anchovy stock, curry powder, lemon grass, polygonum leaves, torch ginger bud and dried sour fruit to a boil in a large pot.
- Add dried prawns, dried anchovies, finely ground ingredients and kerisik. Simmer over low heat for 30 minutes. Add fish flakes, coconut milk and salt to taste.
- To serve, put a handful of laksa noodles in a bowl, add gravy and garnish.

Mee Rebus

Of the many versions of 'mee rebus' using either sweet potatoes or potatoes to thicken the gravy, this is one of my favourites. It requires time to prepare but the prawn crisps and crisp-fried shallots can be done in advance and refrigerated in air-tight containers.

Gravy Ingredients

Sweet potatoes	500 g (orange-coloured variety), skinned, peeled and cut into large chunks
Fresh chicken or anchovy stock	1¹/₂ litres, (refer to page 18 and 113)
Sunflower or corn oil	3 Tbsp
Salt	5 tsp
Sugar	2 tsp
Small prawns	100 g, peeled and seasoned with ¹/₄ tsp salt and ¹/₄ tsp white pepper
Fresh coconut cream	100 ml (refer to page 119)

Finely Ground

Dried chillies	12 large, seeded and soaked to soften
Shallots	16, peeled
Garlic	2 cloves, peeled
Candlenuts	5
Young galangal	2.5-cm knob, peeled
Turmeric	5-cm knob, peeled
Preserved soy bean paste	1 tsp
Coriander powder	1 Tbsp, roasted

Mee Rebus Ingredients

Bean sprouts	300 g, tailed and scalded
Yellow noodles	600 g, scalded
Eggs	4 hard-boiled, shelled and quartered
Potatoes	2, boiled, peeled and cubed
Firm tofu	3 pieces, fried and diced

Garnish

Green chillies	2, sliced
Crisp-fried shallots	4 Tbsp
Prawn crisps*	
Kalamansi limes	6–8, halved

To Make the Gravy

- Steam sweet potatoes in a heatproof dish over rapidly boiling water for 30 minutes or until soft. Blend with 750 ml chicken or anchovy stock into a purée. Set aside.
- Meanwhile heat the oil in a large deep saucepan and fry finely ground ingredients over medium heat until fragrant. Gradually pour in the sweet potato purée and the remaining chicken or anchovy stock and bring to the boil. Add salt and sugar and stir well.

- Add the seasoned prawns and coconut cream. Bring to the boil and remove from heat. Reheat the gravy again just before serving.

To Serve
- Place some bean sprouts and noodles in a serving bowl. Add a few pieces of hard-boiled egg, potatoes and tofu. Top with gravy.
- Garnish with green chillies, crisp-fried shallots, prawn crisps and 1–2 kalamansi halves.

⁕ Prawn Crisps

Ingredients

Rice flour	100 g
Plain flour	50 g
Cornflour	1 Tbsp
Coconut milk	350 ml, extracted from 175 g grated coconut and 350 ml water
Egg	1, beaten
Dried baby prawns	30 g
Oil for deep-frying	

Finely Ground

Coriander powder	1 tsp
Garlic	2 cloves, peeled
Lesser galangal	3-cm knob
Candlenuts	5
Salt	1¹/₂ tsp

Method
- Sift rice flour, plain flour and cornflour into a basin. Add finely ground ingredients and mix well.
- Combine coconut milk and beaten egg and blend well into flour mixture until the batter is smooth. Strain into another basin. Add dried baby prawns and mix well.
- Heat oil in a wok. Spread 1 Tbsp batter on side of wok. Ladle oil over and when set, ease it into the oil. Cook until golden brown. Drain on absorbent kitchen paper. Cool and store in airtight container.

Note: You can use either white or yellow sweet potatoes (but not the purple variety) if the orange-coloured sweet potatoes are not available. However, to keep the colour an attractive vibrant orange, use more fresh turmeric root.

Spicy Egg Noodles

This dish takes only minutes to prepare and is great for when you have unexpected guests.

Ingredients

Corn oil	2 Tbsp
Firm tofu	2 pieces
Garlic	3 cloves, peeled and chopped
Ginger	4 thick slices, peeled and chopped
Red chilli	1, seeded and chopped
Sichuan preserved vegetables	100 g, finely chopped
Chinese rice wine	2 Tbsp
Chilli bean sauce	2 Tbsp
Sesame paste or finely ground sesame seeds	1 Tbsp
Thick soy sauce	$^1/_2$ Tbsp
Sugar	1 Tbsp
Fresh chicken stock	500 ml (refer to page 18)
Cornflour	1 tsp, mixed with 1 Tbsp water
Bean sprouts	125 g, rinsed and tailed
Fresh or packet egg noodles	450 g

Garnish

Spring onion	1, chopped

Method

- Heat oil in a large saucepan and fry the tofu on both sides until golden brown. Remove, slice and set aside.
- In the same saucepan, stir-fry garlic, ginger and red chilli until fragrant. Add Sichuan preserved vegetables and cook for 1–2 minutes.
- Splash in wine. Add chilli bean sauce, sesame paste or ground sesame seeds, soy sauce and sugar. Pour in chicken stock and bring to the boil. Reduce heat and simmer for 3 minutes. Thicken with cornflour mixture.
- Scald the bean sprouts in a large pot of boiling water for 30 seconds. Drain and place on a serving dish.
- Scald dried noodles for 3 minutes or according to instructions. Drain well and place over bean sprouts. (For fresh egg noodles, scald for a minute, drain and cool in a basin of cold water. Stir with chopsticks to get rid of excess starch. Drain and place over bean sprouts.)
- Ladle sauce over and top with tofu and a sprinkling of chopped spring onions before serving.

Spicy Stir-fried Noodles with Tofu

A light noodle dish that is ideal for days when you want to go vegetarian.

Ingredients

Sunflower or corn oil	60 ml
Semi-soft tofu	2 pieces, halved and sliced
Onion	1, peeled and sliced
Cabbage	200 g, cut into 2 x 5-cm pieces
Mustard greens	3–4 stalks, cut into 6-cm lengths (separate the leaves from the stalks)
Pre-fried tofu	10 pieces
Tomato	1, cut into 8 wedges
Yellow noodles	600 g, scalded for 3 seconds
Bean sprouts	150 g, tailed

Sauce

Light soy sauce	2 Tbsp
Meat curry powder	2 Tbsp, preferably for chicken
Bottled tomato ketchup	3 Tbsp
Bottled chilli sauce	2 Tbsp
Salt	$1^1/_2$ tsp
Sugar	$^1/_2$ tsp
White pepper	$^1/_2$ tsp

Garnish

Red chillies	2, seeded and shredded
Kalamansi limes	10, halved

Method

- Heat 3 Tbsp oil in a wok and fry semi-soft tofu until light golden. Set aside.
- Reheat the wok, add the remaining oil and lightly brown the onion. Add cabbage and stir-fry for a few minutes until cabbage is limp. Add the stalks of mustard greens, pre-fried tofu and tomato and mix well.
- Add the noodles. Toss well for 2–3 minutes.
- Pour in the sauce and stir-fry until well combined.
- Add the mustard green leaves, bean sprouts and semi-soft tofu. Mix well.
- Dish out on to a large serving plate and garnish with cut chillies and kalamansi. Serve hot.

Note: The yellow noodles are scalded very briefly to get rid of excess oil. Do this just before you are ready to cook the noodles or they may stick together.

Spaghetti in Tofu Tomato Sauce

A fine blend of flavours, this dish tantalises the taste buds.

Tomato Sauce

Olive oil	2 Tbsp
Large onion	1, peeled and chopped
Garlic	3 cloves, peeled and crushed
Tomatoes	1 can (400 g), chopped
Tomato purée	3 Tbsp
Golden raisins	25 g, soaked in water for 15 minutes and drained
Sultanas	25 g, soaked in water for 15 minutes and drained
Firm tofu	1 piece, diced small
Chicken or mushroom stock	100 ml (refer to page 18 or 20)
Red wine	75 ml
Sugar	$1/_2$ Tbsp
Salt	$1 1/_2$ tsp
Ground black pepper	$1/_2$ tsp
Lemon basil leaves	20, chopped

Breadcrumbs and Pine Nut Mixture

Olive oil	1 Tbsp
Pine nuts	60 g
Garlic	1 clove, peeled and crushed
Fresh white breadcrumbs	60 g
Parsley	1 Tbsp, chopped

Pasta

Spaghetti	150 g
Sunflower or corn oil	1 Tbsp
Pinch of salt	

Method

- To cook the tomato sauce, heat olive oil in a deep saucepan and gently fry the onion and garlic until onion softens. Add chopped tomatoes and tomato purée and bring to the boil. Simmer for 5–8 minutes.
- Add the raisins, sultanas, tofu, chicken or mushroom stock, wine, sugar, salt and pepper. Simmer for 10–15 minutes, stirring occasionally. Add basil. Stir and transfer to a serving dish.
- To cook the breadcrumbs and pine nuts, heat olive oil in a frying pan and fry the pine nuts until they begin to turn golden. Remove from heat and add garlic and breadcrumbs. Fry, stirring until the crumbs turn crisp. Add parsley and return pine nuts to pan. Mix well and transfer to a small serving dish.
- To cook the pasta, boil a saucepan of water with the oil and salt. Put in the spaghetti and cook for 10 minutes or according to the instructions until al-dente. Drain the spaghetti and place on a serving dish.
- Just before serving, add the tomato sauce and mix well. Sprinkle with crispy breadcrumb and pine nut mixture. Serve immediately.

Teriyaki Noodles with Tofu Salmon

Offering a great balance of flavours, this combination of ingredients also makes a healthy meal.

Ingredients

Salmon fillet	350 g
Dried egg noodles	460 g
Firm tofu	3 pieces, cut into 1-cm cubes
Oil for deep-frying	
Sunflower or corn oil	3 Tbsp
Garlic	4 cloves, peeled and sliced
Hot paprika	1 tsp
Fresh oyster mushrooms	50 g, diced
Fresh Enoki mushrooms	100 g, cut into 2-cm lengths
Fresh button mushrooms	10, sliced
Lime juice	extracted from 2 large limes
Canned tomato paste	2 level Tbsp
Fresh chicken stock	3 Tbsp (refer to page 18)
Salt	2 tsp or to taste
Bean sprouts	120 g tailed
Peanuts	2 Tbsp roasted, coarsely ground
Sesame seeds	1 Tbsp, toasted

Marinade

Salt	$1/2$ tsp
White pepper	$1/4$ tsp
Teriyaki sauce	4 Tbsp
Light soy sauce	2 Tbsp
Dashi powder	2 tsp
Sugar	1 tsp

Garnish

Coriander leaves

Method

- Combine marinade ingredients and marinate salmon for 30 minutes. Grill the salmon for 8 minutes. Reserve the marinade for later use.
- Cook the noodles in a large pot of boiling water together with 1 Tbsp sunflower or corn oil until just cooked through. Drain and rinse thoroughly in cold water. Leave in colander to drain.
- Deep-fry the tofu. Remove and drain.
- Heat remaining sunflower or corn oil in a non-stick wok and lightly brown garlic. Add the paprika and all the mushrooms. Cook for 1 minute.
- Add the lime juice, tomato paste, reserved marinade, chicken stock and salt. Stir and bring to a quick boil.
- Add the noodles and toss with chopsticks. Add the bean sprouts and stir until just cooked.
- Remove to a serving dish. Slice the salmon and place on top of the noodles. Sprinkle peanuts and sesame seeds over noodles. Garnish with coriander leaves and serve.

Note: Dashi is a Japanese soup stock. It can be made instantly by mixing Dashi powder with water. It is available at leading supermarkets.

Thai Fried Chilli Tofu with Vermicelli

The blending of garlic, lemon lime, chillies and fish sauce adds piquancy to this Thai-style noodle dish.

Ingredients

Dried fine vermicelli	400 g, soaked in water for 20 minutes until soft
Small prawns	150 g, peeled or 150 g chicken fillet, diced small
Salt	$^1/_2$ tsp
White pepper	$^1/_4$ tsp
Sunflower or corn oil	60 ml
Shallots	6, peeled and sliced
Garlic	4 cloves, peeled and sliced
Dried prawns	50 g, rinsed and coarsely pounded
Preserved radish	60 g, finely chopped
Chilli paste*	$^1/_2$ portion
Dried prawn paste granules	1 Tbsp
Firm tofu	3 pieces, sliced
Sunflower or corn oil	1 Tbsp
Eggs	2, beaten
Sugar	2 Tbsp
Bean sprouts	300 g
Chives	12 stalks, cut into 2-cm lengths
Spring onions	3, cut into 2-cm lengths
Bird's eye chillies	10, chopped

Sauce

Lemon juice	3 Tbsp
Fish sauce	60 ml
Water	120 ml

Garnish

Peanuts	3 Tbsp, roasted and coarsely blended
Spring onions	2 Tbsp, chopped
Coriander leaves	2 Tbsp, chopped
Red chillies	1–2, cut into strips

Method

- Drain the vermicelli after 20 minutes and set aside. Season prawns or chicken with salt and pepper. Set aside.
- Heat the 60 ml oil in a wok and lightly brown shallots and garlic. Add dried prawns and preserved radish and fry until fragrant.
- Add the chilli paste and dried prawn paste granules and fry for 1 minute. Add the seasoned prawns or chicken and toss until the meat changes colour. Add the tofu and cook for 1–2 minutes.
- Push the fried ingredients to one side of the pan. Drizzle 1 Tbsp sunflower or corn oil and quickly add the beaten egg. Once the egg begins to set, scramble the egg until cooked.
- Combine the sauce ingredients and add to wok together with the sugar. Add bean sprouts, chives, spring onions and chillies and toss for 30 seconds. Combine with fried ingredients.
- Add vermicelli and toss mixture vigorously with the help of a spatula and chopsticks, until well mixed, cooked and dry.
- Arrange on a serving dish and garnish with peanuts, spring onions, coriander leaves and chillies.

* Chilli Paste

Ingredients

Dried chillies	10, seeded and soaked until soft
Onions	2 medium, peeled and cut into 2-cm chunks
Garlic	6 large cloves, peeled
Dried prawn paste granules	2 tsp
Dried prawns	50 g, rinsed
Tamarind juice	1 tsp tamarind pulp, mixed with 60 ml water and strained
Sunflower or corn oil	3 Tbsp
Brown sugar	1 Tbsp

Method

- Blend all the ingredients, except brown sugar, in a liquidiser until fine.
- Pour into a non-stick saucepan and cook, stirring all the time, over low heat for 8–10 minutes until fragrant. Add brown sugar and stir. Remove from heat and set aside to cool.
- The chilli paste can be stored, frozen, for several weeks.

Glossary

Index

Weights & Measures

SAUCES

Abalone Sauce
A thick brown sauce made from abalone extract and flavoured with seasoning.

Chilli Bean Sauce
A thick dark reddish sauce made from chillies, garlic and seasoning. It is hot and spicy with an aromatic flavour of fermented soya beans. It is easily available in leading supermarkets, usually in jars. Once opened, it is best stored in the refrigerator.

Hoisin Sauce
A thick and brownish red sauce for Chinese cooking widely used in Hong Kong. Made from soy beans, vinegar, sugar and spices, it is sweet and spicy. It is sold in jars and should be kept in the refrigerator.

XO Sauce
A Hong Kong style sauce rich in flavour made of dried scallops, dried prawns, salted fish, sole fish and an assortment of spices and chillies. The name is adopted from XO brandy to indicate a premium and extraordinary rich sauce.

INGREDIENTS

Arrowhead (Tong Ku)
Arrowhead is a bulb with a cream-brown husk, larger than the water chestnut. When peeled, it reveals a plump white disc of flesh with a texture similar to the potato. It is imported from China, and it can be found in abundance in supermarkets and wet markets during the Chinese New Year period. It is used for stir-frying, braising and for making into chips, a popular tid-bit during Chinese New Year.

Tofu (Weight and Sizes)
Tofu does not come in standard sizes and can vary in weight depending on water content. The weights and sizes are given in this book as a guide. Variance in weight of up to 50–60 g for individual tofu pieces will not affect the outcome of the recipes.

Black Moss (Fatt Choy)
Also known as "hair vegetable" because it resembles a mass of black fine hair, black moss is dried seaweed. The Chinese name fatt choy literally means prosperity. The auspicious vegetable is a must-have during the Chinese New Year meals, as it is believed to bring luck and prosperity for the year ahead.

Bonito Flakes
Seasoned dried tuna flakes, bonito flakes are packed in small sachets and are available at leading supermarkets.

Chinese Chard (Bok Choy)
This Chinese vegetable is also known as pak choy. It has crunchy stalks and large leaves and is stir-fried, steamed or used in soups. Small heads are known as baby Chinese chard.

Chinese Dried Black Mushrooms (Tung Ku)
This mushroom is related to the Japanese shiitake mushroom. Reconstitute before use by soaking in warm water for at least 30 minutes. When soft, drain and squeeze lightly to get rid of excess liquid. It is available packed or loose. Choose pieces with a thick umbrella-like cap, as they are meatier and tastier. Trim off the stems and retain for use in making stock.

Cloud Ear (Wan Yee) and Wood Ear Fungus (Mok Yee)
Cloud ear fungus is a small and wrinkled dried black fungus. When soaked, they expand to look like clouds, hence the name. They have very little taste and aroma but are valued for their crunchy texture. The larger variety is wood ear fungus. They are thicker, crunchier, and more expensive. When soaked for at least 20 minutes, both the cloud ear and wood ear fungus will expand 4–5 times their original size. Rinse well and cut away the hard portions before use. Cloud ear and wood ear fungus keep indefinitely when stored in a cool dry place.

Coconut Cream (Patti Santan)
This is pure coconut milk obtained from squeezing grated coconut in muslin cloth without adding water. A large grated coconut, about 350 g in weight, will yield approximately 250 ml coconut cream. Nowadays the tedious task of squeezing fresh grated coconut can be done away with as coconut cream is readily available in wet markets and supermarkets. Add water to vary the thickness as required.

Dried Radish (Choy Poh)
A salted and dried radish cut into small pieces or minced. It is used to flavour steamed and stir-fried dishes, and is also used in omelettes. It goes well with porridge.

Dried Sour Fruit (Asam Gelugur)
This is sun-dried fruit of the asam gelugur tree. It is used in soups and curries and is favoured for its sour taste.

Enoki Mushroom
This mushroom is available fresh or canned, and is sold in wet markets and supermarkets. It is whitish in colour and has a pinhead cap. With a mild flavour with a smooth delicate crunch, enoki mushrooms are often used in soups or stir-fried and braised dishes.

Galangal (Lam Keong)
Greater galangal (called *lengkuas* in Malaysia, *laos* in Indonesia and *kha* in Thailand) has a delicate flavour and is normally used fresh in Malaysian, Indonesian and Thai cooking. Lesser galangal or aromatic ginger (called *cekur* in Malaysia and Singapore) is a smaller variety of galangal. It has a strong flavour and therefore only a small quantity needs to be used.

Gingko Nut (Pak Kor)
A yellow almond-shaped nut used as a savoury stuffing or in sweet and savoury soups. It is soft and tender with a delicate flavour. The shell, inner skin and center vein are bitter and have to be removed before use.

Hong Kong Starch
A superior quality starch flour, Hong Kong Starch has a bleach-white colour. It is used for thickening sauces and soups. It can be substituted with tapioca or potato flour.

Indonesian Bitter Melinjau Cracker (Keropok Melinjau or Emping)
This is a thin, flat and round cream-coloured cracker. The 'melinjau' fruit is cut into slices, flattened and dried, and then deep fried in hot oil as you would for prawn crackers or chips. As its name implies, the *melinjau* crackers have a slight bitter taste. They go well with curry noodles and are often eaten as a tid-bit with drinks.

Pickled Vegetable (Tung Choy)
These are small brown pieces of pickled garlic stems. A traditional favourite of the Teochews, this pickled vegetable is usually sold in brown or black coloured earthen jars. Today it is also available packed in plastic. Used mainly in soups, the vegetable has to be rinsed in several changes of water to reduce its saltiness before use.

Pointed Pepper Leaf (Daun Kaduk)
Native to Borneo and Indonesia, the leaf is now widely cultivated in South-east Asia and China. It is a tall-branched herb with a hairy stem. The thin, oval leaves smell and taste slightly pungent. In Malaysia, they are eaten as a vegetable, either raw or blanched in boiling water as an appetiser.

Preserved Black Beans (Hak Tau See)
These are small black beans fermented with salt and spices. They have a pleasant aroma when stir-fried and are used sparingly in meat and seafood dishes. Rinse or soak in water for 5–10 minutes before use. They are sold either whole or coarsely chopped in small plastic packages.

Preserved Prawns (Cencaluk)
This is made from small, fine prawns, which can be found in the Straits of Melaka. Hot boiled rice and brandy is added to the prawns to help the fermentation process before the mixture is bottled. The mixture takes 2–3 days to mature. Preserved prawns are eaten as relish by adding sliced fresh shallots, chillies and lime juice.

Salted Cabbage (Harm Choy)
This is green stem pickled with salt. The vegetable should be washed and soaked in water to reduce its saltiness before use. It can be fried with meat or used in soups, and goes especially well with duck.

Sesame Oil
Dark sesame oil is extracted from roasted sesame seeds. It has a rich nutty taste and a smoky aroma. The oil is dark in colour and has a cloudy appearance. It is used sparingly in recipes as even a small amount gives off an intense aroma.

Shiitake Mushroom
Brown in colour with a wild woody aroma, shiitake mushrooms have a cracked floral cap. They are a good source of vitamin B and ergosterol, a form of vitamin D. It is available fresh or dried. Good quality shiitake mushrooms are thick and have firm-fleshed caps. The dried mushroom should be soaked in water for at least an hour to soften before using. The tough stem is usually cut and discarded before cooking.

Sunflower Oil
Made from sunflower seeds, sunflower oil has a pleasant taste and clear consistency. It keeps well and it is often used in place of corn or groundnut oil.

Sichuan Preserved Vegetable (Char Choy)
This is preserved Chinese radish pickled in salt and chillies. The olive green vegetable should be washed to get rid of the chilli powder coating and then soaked in water to reduce its saltiness before use.

Wakame
A brown algae found in the temperate waters off the coasts of Japan, China and Korea. When cooked, it turns into a beautiful olive green. Although it is still harvested wild, much of wakame available today is cultivated. When harvested, the seaweed is washed, then hung to dry in the sun for several days until it is completely dry and crisp. Dried wakame is reconstituted by soaking in water for a couple of minutes. It becomes slippery smooth in texture with a strong flavour of the ocean. It tastes especially good in soups and salads.

INDEX

WEIGHTS & MEASURES

Quantities for this book are given in Metric and American (spoon and cup) measures. Standard spoon and cup measurements used are: 1 tsp = 5 ml, 1 dsp = 10 ml, 1 Tbsp = 15 ml, 1 cup = 250 ml. All measures are level unless otherwise stated.

LIQUID AND VOLUME MEASURES

Metric	Imperial	American
5 ml	$1/6$ fl oz	1 tsp
10 ml	$1/3$ fl oz	1 dsp
15 ml	$1/2$ fl oz	1 Tbsp
60 ml	2 fl oz	$1/4$ cup (4 Tbsp)
85 ml	$2^1/2$ fl oz	$1/3$ cup
90 ml	3 fl oz	$3/8$ cup (6 Tbsp)
125 ml	4 fl oz	$1/2$ cup
180 ml	6 fl oz	$3/4$ cup
250 ml	8 fl oz	1 cup
300 ml	10 fl oz ($1/2$ pint)	$1^1/4$ cups
375 ml	12 fl oz	$1^1/2$ cups
435 ml	14 fl oz	$1^3/4$ cups
500 ml	16 fl oz	2 cups
625 ml	20 fl oz (1 pint)	$2^1/2$ cups
750 ml	24 fl oz ($1^1/5$ pints)	3 cups
1 litre	32 fl oz ($1^3/5$ pints)	4 cups
1.25 litres	40 fl oz (2 pints)	5 cups
1.5 litres	48 fl oz ($2^2/5$ pints)	6 cups
2.5 litres	80 fl oz (4 pints)	10 cups

DRY MEASURES

Metric	Imperial
30 g	1 ounce
45 g	$1^1/2$ ounces
55 g	2 ounces
70 g	$2^1/2$ ounces
85 g	3 ounces
100 g	$3^1/2$ ounces
110 g	4 ounces
125 g	$4^1/2$ ounces
140 g	5 ounces
280 g	10 ounces
450 g	16 ounces (1 pound)
500 g	1 pound, $1^1/2$ ounces
700 g	$1^1/2$ pounds
800 g	$1^3/4$ pounds
1 kg	2 pounds, 3 ounces
1.5 kg	3 pounds, $4^1/2$ ounces
2 kg	4 pounds, 6 ounces

OVEN TEMPERATURE

	°C	°F	Gas Regulo
Very slow	120	250	1
Slow	150	300	2
Moderately slow	160	325	3
Moderate	180	350	4
Moderately hot	190/200	370/400	5/6
Hot	210/220	410/440	6/7
Very hot	230	450	8
Super hot	250/290	475/550	9/10

LENGTH

Metric	Imperial
0.5 cm	$1/4$ inch
1 cm	$1/2$ inch
1.5 cm	$3/4$ inch
2.5 cm	1 inch